GERMAN SCHAUSS'S

SPEED GUITAR

Learn Lightning-Fast Alternate Picking and Flawless Coordination

Stream or download the video and audio content
for this book. For more information, please see
the insert card on the inside back cover.

Alfred Music
P.O. Box 10003
Van Nuys, CA 91410-0003
alfred.com

Copyright © MMXVII by Alfred Music
All rights reserved. Printed in USA.

ISBN-10: 1-4706-2981-X (Book & Online Video/Audio)
ISBN-13: 978-1-4706-2981-6 (Book & Online Video/Audio)

Cover photo of German Schauss © Alfred Music

 Alfred Cares. Contents printed on environmentally responsible paper.

CONTENTS

ABOUT THE AUTHOR

German Schauss is a guitarist, composer, author, and educator who has taught at Berklee College of Music and other international music schools. He also performs and tours as the leader of his own band and with other internationally known artists. German writes music for commercials, television, and video games, and was named one of the 50 fastest guitarists of all time by *Guitar World* magazine. He has written numerous books for Alfred Music, including *Shredding Bach*, *Shredding Paganini*, *Shredding the Composers*, and *Serious Shred: Advanced Techniques*. German also writes the popular monthly column "Instant Shredding" for Germany's biggest guitar magazine, *Gitarre & Bass*.

German uses and proudly endorses: Schecter Guitars, Bogner Amps, Kemper Amps, Rocktron, PreSonus, Native Instruments, Maxon, Morley, Dunlop, Voodoo Labs, DiMarzio, Zoom, Tremol-No, D'Addario Strings, Planet Waves, MakeMusic, and Pedaltrain products.

For more about German Schauss and his music, please visit: www.germanschauss.com

ACKNOWLEDGEMENTS

I would like to thank my family, friends, and fans around the world for their support, positive thoughts, and love—you are all an inspiration to me! Additionally, a big thank you to Nat Gunod, Link Harnsberger, and the team at Alfred Music for their support and help.

INTRODUCTION

Developing great picking technique is one of the most challenging undertakings for any guitarist. This book will help you develop your picking technique and speed through various technical and musical approaches. You will not just learn licks but also understand how to develop your musical vocabulary to further your technique and knowledge. This is all with the end goal of becoming a great guitar player and musician. The ideas and examples in this book can be used and applied to any style of music.

Picking Technique

Some of the most common questions in dealing with alternate picking are related to how you hold the pick: How should I angle my hand? Should I only use wrist movement, or can I incorporate some forearm movement? A long time ago, I analyzed the picking technique of guitar players and created a spreadsheet with details on movement, hand placement, pick type, and many other categories. I really wanted to understand how one could achieve great speed and precision, and was hoping to isolate the one thing that everyone had in common. Unfortunately, I mostly found disappointment. Every one of my favorite players was different and had their own technique and approach. However, I did notice one thing that everyone had in common, which was a total rhythmic command over every phrase or idea. That led me to understand that not knowing the correct phrasing or rhythm would lead to mismatched synchronization between the left and right hands. Furthermore, I learned that understanding your body will lead you to naturally find an appropriate way to employ alternate picking—or any other technique—without limitation or waste of energy and time.

Practicing in Front of a Mirror

Speaking of waste of energy, here's a practice tip for you. Try to monitor and observe your left- and right-hand movements in front of a mirror. You can minimize the motion of your fretting hand and develop synchronization via a mirror. This method will also allow you to observe your entire body, not just your left or right hand. Plus, you can always practice your performance moves and guitar faces.

Building up good technique and practice habits will take time and a lot of work, but when you set goals, organize your schedule, and have a clear direction, you can achieve anything!

–German Schauss

 Companion audio recordings are included to help you interpret the rhythm and feel of the musical examples in this book. Follow along with the recordings to make learning more enjoyable and meaningful. The symbol to the left appears next to every example with an audio track.

WARM-UP AND COORDINATION EXERCISES

To obtain great picking technique and to be able to pick as fast as possible, it is important to develop muscle memory and a good vocabulary of patterns and phrases. Warming up is one of the most important parts of your practice session or pre-concert routine, enabling your hands to synchronize and be prepared.

In this chapter, you will find a series of warm-up exercises and strategies to prepare you for all the upcoming challenges.

DANCING FINGERS

Warming up can be a very time- and labor-intensive part of your practice. It is important that you use your time wisely and not spend your warm-up focused on exercises. The following is a fun and challenging idea that uses all your left-hand fingers in different rhythms. The objective is to play the same note on the same string and fret, but use a different finger each time you play it. Additionally, you'll be playing it with different rhythms, following the sequence of the rhythm pyramid: from whole notes to half notes to quarter notes to eighth notes to triplets and finally to 16th notes. Here's the basic idea.

Ex. 1 Track 1

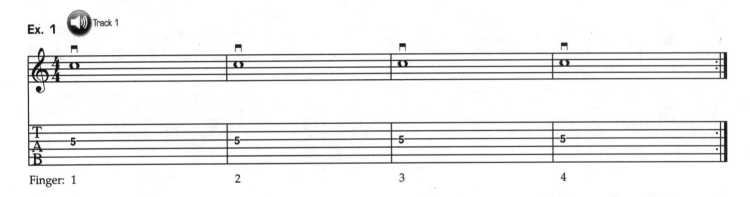

Finger: 1   2   3   4

Now onto half notes:

Ex. 2 Track 2

Now, let's start with quarter notes, then subdivide into eighth notes, eighth-note triplets, and 16th notes.

Ex. 3 Track 3

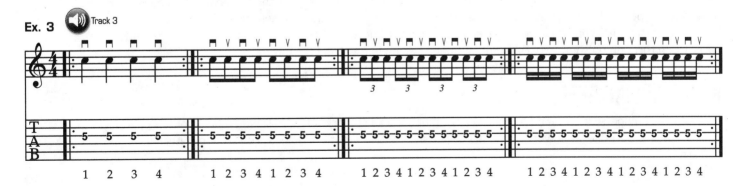

Exercise 4 is a great picking-coordination builder as it mixes up different rhythms. It's based on a simple chromatic scale idea that is played in position.

You'll use all four fingers in the given position and simply stay in position when crossing over to the next string, leaving one chromatic note out of the scale.

Ex. 4 Track 4

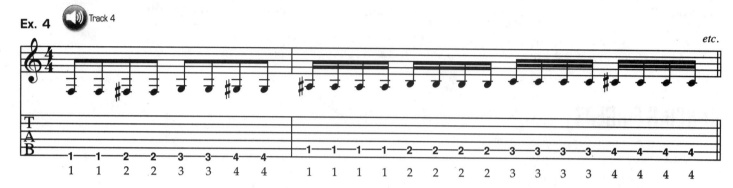

Let's mix it up with some triplets.

Ex. 5 Track 5

Always use a metronome when you practice, setting it to a slow tempo to start. All of these exercises are for warming up, so you want to start slow and gradually bring it up to a medium tempo. For example, start at 60 BPM and increase slowly to 120 BPM.

UNDERSTANDING THE EXAMPLES

As you proceed in this book, you will encounter a unique style of notation that does not specify rhythm. In this system, there are no time signatures and no stems or beams to tell you whether you're playing eighths, 16ths, or triplets. Instead of conventional bar lines, dotted bar lines are used to delineate and highlight note groupings. If there is a three-note pattern, there will be a dotted bar line every three notes; four-note groupings will have a dotted bar line every four notes, etc. These examples are not about rhythm or tempo but, instead, about speed development through practicing melodic patterns across the strings up and down the fretboard. Focus on being able to play the patterns anywhere on the guitar, in any key, with any scale, forward or backward, ascending or descending.

You may notice almost any melodic pattern can be extended to travel across all the strings and frets in every key (e.g., A pattern that starts on the 1st fret of the 6th string can be extended to end at the 20th fret of the 1st string). Writing out every sequence through the entire range of the guitar would require thousands of pages! In this book, we may start a sequence for you in one example and finish it in the beginning of the next. Your goal will be to learn and understand the patterns and sequences provided and carry them through on your own. Remember, speed begins in the mind.

BASIC PICKING SPEED

Now that your fingers are trained for various combinations, let's work on establishing a basic picking speed. For this purpose, let's work chromatically on all strings and utilize basic three- and four-note patterns.

CHROMATIC TRIPLET RUNS

The first of the following exercises are basic chromatic triplet runs in variations. Set the metronome to a slow tempo at first to establish a baseline. Pay close attention to the picking directions here as these will change from string to string. Play this idea up to the 12th fret and then descend.

Three-Note Ascending Pattern: Ascending Sequence
This pattern should be repeated across all six strings, moving up one fret at each change of direction, until the 12th position is reached.

Ex. 6A Track 6

Three-Note Descending Pattern: Descending Sequence
This is an example of us finishing a sequence for you. When the sequence from Ex. 6A reaches the 12th position, change the pattern so that three notes descend in a sequence across the strings, moving down a fret at each change in direction.

Ex. 6B Track 7

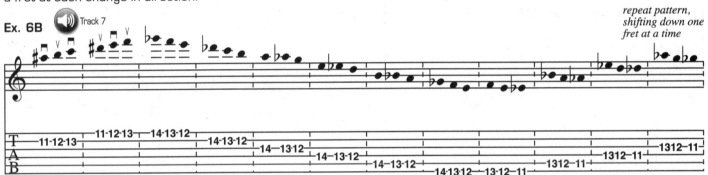

Chromatic Triplet Variations
Here's a variation of the previous concept:

Combining Three-Note Ascending and Descending Patterns: Ascending Sequence

Ex. 7A Track 8

Combining Three-Note Ascending and Descending Patterns: Descending Sequence
Ex. 7B shows the end of the sequence begun in Ex. 7A, and the beginning of the descending sequence.

Ex. 7B Track 9

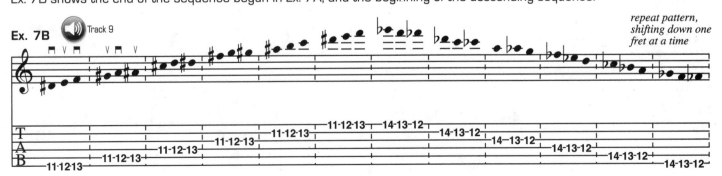

STRING SKIPPING WARM-UPS

Let's introduce some string skipping to our previous concepts. Make sure to keep string noise to a minimum when skipping strings, and pay close attention to your alternate picking. Remember, start slow and keep track of your metronome markings.

String Skipping Ascending Three-Note Pattern: Ascending Sequence

Ex. 8A   Track 10

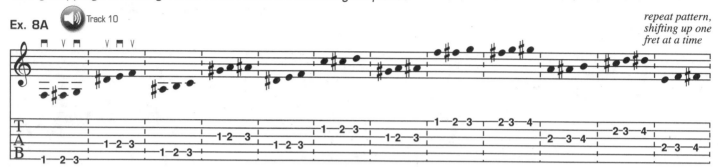

repeat pattern, shifting up one fret at a time

String Skipping Descending Three-Note Pattern: Descending Sequence

Ex. 8B   Track 11

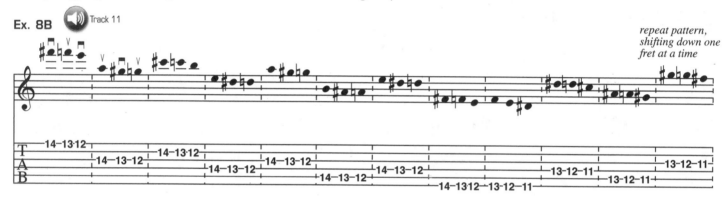

repeat pattern, shifting down one fret at a time

String-Skipping Variations

Here's a variation:

Combining Ascending and Descending Three-Note Pattern: Ascending Sequence

Ex. 9A   Track 12

Combining Descending and Ascending Three-Note Pattern: Descending Sequence

Ex. 9B   Track 13

FOUR-NOTE-PER-STRING CHROMATIC LINES

The following exercises are similar to Exs. 6–9, except they now feature four-note patterns that can be felt as 16th notes (or as eighth notes). Remember, start out slowly, and make sure your picking is controlled and in sync with your fretting hand.

Four-Note Ascending Pattern: Ascending Sequence

Ex. 10A   Track 14

etc.

Four-Note Ascending Pattern: Descending Sequence

Ex. 10B   Track 15

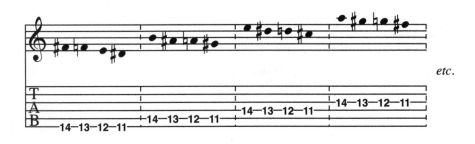

etc.

Four-Note-per-String Chromatic Line Variations
Combining Ascending and Descending Four-Note-per-String Patterns: Ascending Sequence

Ex. 11A  Track 16

Combining Descending and Ascending Four-Note-per-String Patterns: Descending Sequence

Ex. 11B  Track 17

CHROMATIC STRING SKIPPING RUNS

Let's introduce string skipping to the concept we just covered. Carefully work the following chromatic ideas up and down the neck. Start slowly and pay close attention to finger-motion economy when lifting your fingers off the fretboard.

String Skipping Ascending Four-Note Pattern: Ascending Sequence

Ex. 12A   Track 18

etc.

String Skipping Descending Four-Note Pattern: Descending Sequence

Ex. 12B   Track 19

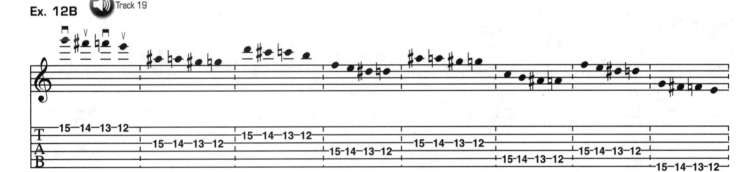

etc.

Variations on Chromatic String Skipping Runs
Combining Ascending and Descending Four-Note Patterns: Ascending Sequence

Ex. 13A  Track 20

etc.

Combining Descending and Ascending Four-Note Patterns: Descending Sequence

Ex. 13B  Track 21

etc.

THE ART OF DEVELOPING PATTERNS AND SEQUENCES

Patterns and sequences of *motives* (short melodic ideas that are repeated and/or sequenced) are an important part of melodic playing and improvisation. Throughout this book, different patterns and sequences will be used to advance and push your speed picking skills by developing a musical vocabulary that not only furthers your technical prowess, but also your motivic/melodic thinking. We can derive several additional patterns from any motive using various melodic devices. Three basic devices are *retrograde*, *inversion*, and *retrograde-inversion*.

DEVICES FOR VARYING A MOTIVE

Let's say your basic idea, what I call *prime*, consists of a pattern of three continuous notes ascending. We can apply inversion, retrograde, and retrograde-inversion to this idea to create three new motives.

Prime (Basic Idea)
Prime is an ascending three-note motive in an ascending sequence.

Ex. 14A  Track 22

Inversion
Invert the direction of the sequence, and descend instead of ascend.

Ex. 14B Track 23

Retrograde
Retrograde means backwards, so we can reverse the actual motive itself, so it goes in the opposite direction. In this case, it goes down instead of up.

Ex. 14C Track 24

Retrograde-Inversion
Not only can we reverse the direction of the motive, but we can invert the direction of the overall sequence.

Ex. 14D Track 25

Furthermore, these devices can be combined as ascending and descending—or descending and ascending—giving you four additional sets of sequences. So, for each idea, you should be able to develop a total of eight possibilities.

You can apply these devices to chromatic, pentatonic, major, and minor scales, as well as arpeggios. Additionally, this principle is also used to develop tone rows in serial music, and of course you can compose your own motives and apply these devices to them.

APPLYING THE MELODIC DEVICES

The following examples show you all the possible pentatonic- and major-scale movements, using the devices described on the previous page (inversion, retrograde, and retrograde inversion). All exercises can be played in any position on the fretboard. We use the 5th position here since it is the most accessible and easiest position on the guitar for the A Minor Pentatonic, C Major, and G Dorian scales.

The prime (basic idea) and retrograde-inversion variation will be provided. Other possibilities are expressed with *pattern numbers* (see below) and scale degrees. Try to memorize these sequences—both with your ears and fingers—as they are an integral part of music. All exercises are to be played with strict alternate picking. Practice each idea slowly and with a metronome to monitor your speed and progress.

Speed, Musical Thinking, and Practice

The goal with this book is to condition your fingers to naturally respond to the musical vocabulary you develop from the practice of melodic-pattern variations—speed will be a secondary benefit. With each new exercise, set your metronome to a medium tempo, like 90–120 BPM, before pushing it. Establish a practice routine where you rotate and exchange different scale exercises, eventually covering all the patterns or ideas within a few days or a week. Also, sing and memorize these patterns so that you can easily recognize and adapt them for other scales or arpeggios. Music is a multifaceted art, and you need to practice the various aural ways it can be perceived as well as produced. All this will help you to become a well-rounded musician. Remember, this is just technical work, so you shouldn't spend too much of your practice time on it and tire out your hands before working on other important materials.

PATTERN NUMBERS

This book makes extensive use of scale patterns, and we will use numbers, called *pattern numbers*, to relate them. Here's how the pattern numbers work: Every scale has formula numbers. For example, the scale tones for the minor pentatonic scale are 1, ♭3, 4, 5, and ♭7. The minor pentatonic scale is a five-note scale, so our pattern numbers will be 1, 2, 3, 4, 5, where 1=1, ♭3=2, 4=3, 5=4, and ♭7=5. Please note that the pattern numbers are *not* formula numbers, scale degrees, finger numbers, or fret numbers, but an independent system unique to this book.

The advantage to using pattern numbers is that a pattern learned with, say, a minor pentatonic scale, can then be applied to another scale with an entirely different set of scale degrees. For example, consider this scale pattern:

1–2–3, 2–3–4, 3–4–5, 4–5–1

Here it is applied to an A Minor Pentatonic scale:

Ex. 15 Track 26

It can also be applied to a C Major scale:

Ex. 16 Track 27

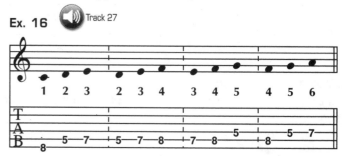

This is the pattern applied to a G Dorian scale:

Ex. 17 Track 28

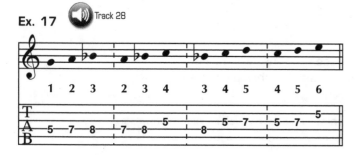

All three of the examples above have unique fingerings, and the scales all have different formula numbers, but all three also use the same scale pattern, 1–2–3, 2–3–4, etc.

DEVELOPING PICKING SKILLS ACROSS THE FRETBOARD

To further develop your picking skills and speed, it is important to study and practice all possible melodic patterns that can be applied to a two-note-per-string scale, such as the pentatonic scale, or a three-note-per-string scale, like the seven modes of the major scale, the harmonic minor scale, the melodic minor scale, etc.

Let's begin our studies with the two-note-per-string A Minor Pentatonic scale. Keep in mind that the following exercises can also be applied to other pentatonic scales or arpeggios that are organized in two-note-per-string groups.

THE A MINOR PENTATONIC SCALE

If you don't know the traditional minor pentatonic scale and all its positions yet, following are diagrams of the five positions of the A Minor Pentatonic Scale. The five notes of A Minor Pentatonic are: A, C, D, E, and G. The musical formula is as follows:

Scale Tone	Pattern Number
1 (root)	1
♭3	2
4	3
5	4
♭7	5

It is imperative that you know all positions of this basic scale. This will enable you to play easily in all positions on the fretboard. Of course, you can also move this scale to the other 11 keys.

Five Positions of A Minor Pentatonic

Starting from the ♭7th

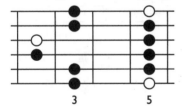

Starting from the Root

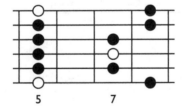

Starting from the ♭3rd

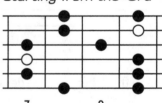

Starting from the 4th

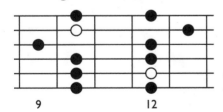

Starting from the 5th

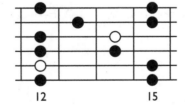

○ = Root

PATTERNS AHEAD!

The scale patterns on pages 16–25 are melodic ascending and descending scale segments from the A Minor Pentatonic scale in three-, four-, five-, and six-note patterns. The ideas are shown with the prime pattern and in retrograde-inversion. Other variations are displayed with scale-tone formulas and pattern numbers. You will decide the note values—whether they are eighths, 16ths, or some kind of triplet. As always, it is important to set the metronome to a comfortable speed and practice these ideas without mistakes before moving on. As always, keep a record of your beginning and top tempo for each exercise. That way, you'll be able to track your progress.

THREE-NOTE PATTERNS

Let's begin with sequencing three-note patterns.

Ex. 18A  Track 29
Prime Pattern: 1–2–3, 2–3–4, 3–4–5, 4–5–1, etc.

Ex. 18B Track 30
Retrograde-Inversion Pattern: 2–1–5, 1–5–4, 5–4–3, 4–3–2, etc.

Now, apply the other melodic devices to the pattern. Remember, play slowly at first and use strict alternate picking.

Ex. 18C
Inversion (Descending from Top String) Pattern: 5–1–2, 4–5–1, 3–4–5, 2–3–4
Scale Degrees: ♭7–1–♭3, 5–♭7–1, 4–5–♭7, ♭3–4–5

Ex. 18D
Retrograde (Ascending from Bottom String) Pattern: 3–2–1, 4–3–2, 5–4–3, 1–5–4
Scale Degrees: 4–♭3–1, 5–4–♭3, ♭7–5–4, 1–♭7–5

Three-Note Variations

Let's take a look at the possibilities of combining the previous two patterns starting with an example of an ascending and descending sequence in groups of three.

Ex. 19A Track 31
Prime (Ascending Three, Descending Three) Pattern: 1–2–3, 4–3–2; 3–4–5, 1–5–4; etc.

And here's the correlating retrograde-inversion sequence.

Ex. 19B Track 32
Retrograde-Inversion (Descending Three, Ascending Three) Pattern: 2–1–5, 4–5–1, 5–4–3, 2–3–4, etc.

Try to develop the remaining two variations based on these formulas.

Ex. 19C
Inversion (Descending from Top String) Pattern: 5–1–2, 1–5–4, 3–4–5, 4–3–2
Scale Degrees: ♭7–1–♭3, 1 ♭7–5, 4–5–♭7, 5–4–♭3

Ex. 19D
Retrograde (Ascending from Bottom String) Pattern: 3–2–1, 2–3–4, 5–4–3, 4–5–1
Scale Degrees: 4–♭3–1, ♭3–4–5, ♭7–5–4, 5–♭7–1

This next example shows how you can create new three-note ideas by playing from one note to another and then returning to the first.

Ex. 20A Track 33
Prime Pattern: 1–2–1, 2–3–2, 3–4–3, 4–5–4, etc.

Ex. 20B Track 34
Retrograde-Inversion Pattern: 2–1–2, 1–5–1, 5–4–5, 4–3–4, etc.

Now, try the remaining two variations based on these patterns:

Ex. 20C
Inversion (Descending from Top String) Pattern: 1–2–1, 5–1–5, 4–5–4, 3–4–3
Scale Degrees: 1–♭3–1, ♭7–1–♭7, 5–♭7–5, 4–5–4

Ex. 20D
Retrograde (Ascending from Bottom String) Pattern: 2–1–2, 3–2–3, 4–3–4, 5–4–5
Scale Degrees: ♭3–1–♭3, 4–♭3–4, 5–4–5, ♭7–5–♭7

Try to develop more combinations and variations based on this idea yourself. It is easy and will help you understand the melodic pattern concept.

FOUR-NOTE PATTERNS

The next sequences use groupings of four. Again, try to develop the remaining variations using the supplied formula. Start out slowly and make sure you are using consistent alternate picking.

Ex. 21A Track 35
Prime Pattern: 1–2–3–4, 2–3–4–5, 3–4–5–1, 4–5–1–2, etc.

Ex. 21B Track 36
Retrograde-Inversion Pattern: 2–1–5–4, 1–5–4–3, 5–4–3–2, 4–3–2–1, etc.

Ex. 21C
Inversion (Descending from Top String) Pattern: 4–5–1–2, 3–4–5–1, 2–3–4–5, 1–2–3–4
Scale Degrees: 5–♭7–1–♭3, 4–5–♭7–1, ♭3–4–5–♭7, 1–♭3–4–5

Ex. 21D
Retrograde (Ascending from Bottom String) Pattern: 4–3–2–1, 5–4–3–2, 1–5–4–3, 2–1–5–4
Scale Degrees: 5–4–♭3–1, ♭7–5–4–♭3, 1–♭7–5–4, ♭3–1–♭7–5

Four-Note Variations
The following exercises are a combination of ascending and descending groups of four.

Ex. 22A Track 37
Prime (Ascending Four, Descending Four) Pattern: 1–2–3–4, 5–4–3–2, 3–4–5–1, 2–1–5–4, etc.

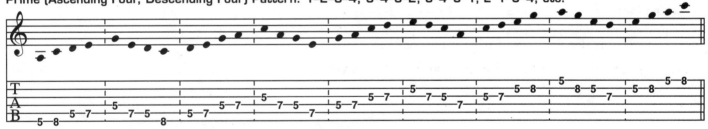

Ex. 22B Track 38
Retrograde-Inversion (Descending Four, Ascending Four) Pattern: 2–1–5–4, 3–4–5–1, 5–4–3–2, 1–2–3–4, etc.

Okay, it's now time for you to develop the remaining variations.

Ex. 22C
Inversion (Descending from Top String) Pattern: 4–5–1–2, 1–5–4–3, 2–3–4–5, 4–3–2–1
Scale Degrees: 5–♭7–1–♭3, 1–♭7–5–4, ♭3–4–5–♭7, 5–4–♭3–1

Ex. 22D
Retrograde (Ascending from Bottom String) Pattern: 4–3–2–1, 2–3–4–5, 1–5–4–3, 4–5–1–2
Scale Degrees: 5–4–♭3–1, ♭3–4–5–♭7, –1–♭7–5–4, 5–♭7–1–♭3

Other Ways to Vary Motives

The following is an interesting variation with a note displacement. Try to develop it further by either adding a note to the beginning of the sequence or by changing the rhythm.

Ex. 23A Track 39
Prime Pattern: 3–1–2–3, 4–2–3–4, 5–3–4–5, 1–4–5–1, etc.

Ex. 23B Track 40
Retrograde-Inversion Pattern: 1–2–1–5, 4–1–5–4, 3–5–4–3, 2–4–3–2, etc.

Below are two more variations of the pattern. Have fun!

Ex. 23C
Descending Pattern: 2–1–5–2, 1–5–4–1, 5–4–3–5, 4–3–2–4

Ex. 23D
Ascending Pattern: 1–2–3–1, 2–3–4–2, 3–4–5–3, 4–5–1–4

Try to continue this idea and develop more variations of your own.

FIVE-NOTE PATTERNS

Of course, there is a lot more to playing sequences than the typical three- and four-note groupings. The following sequences are based on groups of five and will give you a more-modern sound and feel.

Ex. 24A Track 41
Prime Pattern: 1–2–3–4–5, 2–3–4–5–1, 3–4–5–1–2, 4–5–1–2–3, etc.

Ex. 24B Track 42
Retrograde-Inversion Pattern: 2–1–5–4–3, 1–5–4–3–2, 5–4–3–2–1, 4–3–2–1–5, etc.

Here are more variations:

Ex. 24C
Inversion (Descending from Top String) Pattern: 3–4–5–1–2, 2–3–4–5–1, 1–2–3–4–5, 5–1–2–3–4
Scale Degrees: 4–5–♭7–1–♭3, ♭3–4–5–♭7–1, 1–♭3–4–5–♭7, ♭7–1–♭3–4–5

Ex. 24D
Retrograde (Ascending from Bottom String) Pattern: 5–4–3–2–1, 1–5–4–3–2, 2–1–5–4–3, 3–2–1–5–4
Scale Degrees: ♭7–5–4–♭3–1, 1–♭7–5–4–♭3, ♭3–1–♭7–5–4, 4–♭3–1–♭7–5

Let's combine some five-note ideas.

Ex. 25A Track 43
Prime (Ascending Five, Descending Five) Pattern: 1–2–3–4–5, 1–5–4–3–2, 3–4–5–1–2, 3–2–1–5–4, etc.

Ex. 25B Track 44
Retrograde-Inversion (Descending Five, Ascending Five) Pattern: 2–1–5–4–3, 2–3–4–5–1, 5–4–3–2–1, 5–1–2–3–4, etc.

Here are two more variations:

Ex. 25C
Inversion (Descending from Top String) Pattern: 3–4–5–1–2, 1–5–4–3–2, 1–2–3–4–5, 4–3–2–1–5
Scale Degrees: 4–5–♭7–1–♭3, 1–♭7–5–4–♭3, 1–♭3–4–5–7, 5–4–♭3–1–♭7

Ex. 25D
Retrograde (Ascending from Bottom String) Pattern: 5–4–3–2–1, 2–3–4–5–1, 2–1–5–4–3–2, 3–4–5–1–2
Scale Degrees: ♭7–5–4–♭3–1, ♭3–4–5–♭7–1, ♭3–1–♭7–5–4, 5–♭7–1–♭3–4

Here are some more variations on the five-note pattern sequence.

Ex. 26A Track 45
Prime Pattern:
1–2–3–4–5, 3–4–5–1–2, 5–1–2–3–4, 2–3–4–5–1

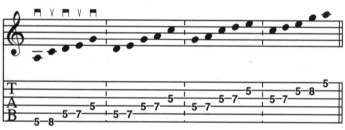

Ex. 26B Track 46
Retrograde-Inversion Pattern:
2–1–5–4–3, 5–4–3–2–1, 3–2–1–5–4, 1–5–4–3–2

Again, try to develop the remaining variations.

Ex. 26C
Descending Pattern: 3–4–5–1–2, 1–2–3–4–5, 4–5–1–2–3, 2–3–4–5–1
Scale Degrees: 4–5–♭7–1–♭3, 1–♭3–4–5–♭7, 5–♭7–1–♭3–4, ♭3–4–5–♭7–1

Ex. 26D
Ascending Pattern: 5–4–3–2–1, 2–1–5–4–3, 4–3–2–1–5, 1–5–4–3–2
Scale Degrees: ♭7–5–4–♭3–1, ♭3–1–♭7–5–4, 5–4–♭3–1–♭7, 1–♭7–5–4–♭3

Five-Note Pattern Combinations

Ex. 27A
Prime (Ascending Five, Descending Five) Pattern:
1–2–3–4–5, 2–1–5–4–3, 5–1–2–3–4, 1–5–4–3–2

Ex. 27B
Retrograde-Inversion (Descending Five, Ascending Five) Pattern:
2–1–5–4–3, 5–1–2–3–4, 3–2–1–5–4, 1–2–3–4–5

Ex. 27C Descending Pattern: 3–4–5–1–2, 5–4–3–2–1, 4–5–1–2–3, 1–5–4–3–2
Scale Degrees: 4–5–♭7–1–♭3, ♭7–5–4–♭3–1, 5–♭7–1–♭3–4, 1–♭7–5–4–♭3

Ex. 27D Ascending Pattern: 5–4–3–2–1, 3–4–5–1–2, 4–3–2–1–5, 2–3–4–5–1
Scale Degrees: ♭7–5–4–♭3–1, 4–5–♭7–1–♭3, 5–4–♭3–1–♭7, ♭3–4–5–♭7–1

SIX-NOTE PATTERNS

Let's try groupings of six. This is a very fluent and contemporary sound.

Ex. 28A Track 47

Prime Pattern: 1–2–3–4–5–1, 2–3–4–5–1–2, 3–4–5–1–2–3, 4–5–1–2–3–4, etc.

Ex. 28B Track 48

Retrograde-Inversion Pattern: 2–1–5–4–3–2, 1–5–4–3–2–1, 5–4–3–2–1–5, 4–3–2–1–5–4, etc.

Following are the other variations:

Ex. 28C

Inversion (Descending from Top String) Pattern: 2–1–5–4–3–2, 1–5–4–3–2–1, 5–4–3–2–1–5, 4–3–2–1–5–4
Scale Degrees: ♭3–4–5–♭7–1–♭3, 1–♭3–4–5–♭7–1, ♭7–1–♭3–4–5–♭7, etc.

Ex. 28D

Retrograde (Ascending from Bottom String) Pattern: 1–5–4–3–2–1, 2–1–5–4–3–2, 3–2–1–5–4–3, 4–3–2–1–5–4
Scale Degrees: 1–♭7–5–4–♭3–1, ♭3–1–♭7–5–4–♭3, 4–♭3–1–♭7–5–4, etc.

Six-Note Variations

Let's combine the prime and retrograde-inversion to create something new.

Ex. 29A Track 49

Prime (Ascending Six, Descending Six) Pattern: 1–2–3–4–5–1, 2–1–5–4–3–2; 3–4–5–1–2–3, 4–3–2–1–5–4; etc.

Ex. 29B Track 50

Retrograde-Inversion (Descending Six, Ascending Six) Pattern: 2–1–5–4–3–2, 1–2–3–4–5–1; 5–4–3–2–1–5, 4–5–1–2–3–4; etc.

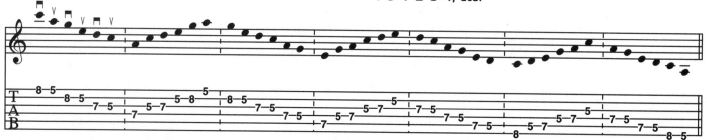

These are the other variations:

Ex. 29C

Inversion (Descending from Top String) Pattern: 2–1–5–4–3–2, 1–2–3–4–5–1, 5–4–3–2–1–5, 4–5–1–2–3–4
Scale Degrees: ♭3–4–5–♭7–1–♭3, 1–♭7–5–4–♭3–1, ♭7–1–♭3–4–5–♭7, etc.

Ex. 29D

Retrograde (Ascending from Bottom String) Pattern: 1–5–4–3–2–1, 2–3–4–5–1–2, 3–2–1–5–4–3, 4–5–1–2–3–4
Scale Degrees: 1–♭7–5–4–♭3–1, ♭3–4–5–♭7–1–♭3, 4–♭3–1–♭7–5–4, etc.

More Six-Note Patterns and Variations
Here are a few different six-note patterns. Develop them further!

Ex. 30A Track 51
Prime: 1–2–3–4–5–1, 3–4–5–1–2–3,
5–1–2–3–4–5, 2–3–4–5–1–2

Ex. 30B Track 52
Retrograde-Inversion: 2–1–5–4–3–2, 5–4–3–2–1–5,
3–2–1–5–4–3, 1–5–4–3–2–1

Here are some more variations of six-note patterns:

Ex. 30C
Inversion (Descending from Top String) Pattern: 2–3–4–5–1–2, 5–1–2–3–4–5, 3–4–5–1–3, 1–2–3–4–5–1

Ex. 30D
Retrograde (Ascending from Bottom String) Pattern: 1–5–4–3–2–1, 3–2–1–5–4–3, 5–4–3–2–1–5, 2–1–5–4–3–2

Ex. 31A
Prime (Ascending Six, Descending Six):
1–2–3–4–5–1, 3–2–1–5–4–3, 5–1–2–3–4–5, 2–1–5–4–3–2

Ex. 31B
Retrograde-Inversion (Descending Six, Ascending Six):
2–1–5–4–3–2, 5–1–2–3–4–5, 3–2–1–5–4–3, 1–2–3–4–5–1

Ex. 31C
Inversion (Descending from Top String) Pattern: 2–3–4–5–1–2, 5–4–3–2–1–5, 3–4–5–1–2–3, 1–5–4–3–2–1

Ex. 30D
Retrograde (Ascending from Bottom String) Pattern: 1–5–4–3–2–1, 3–4–5–1–2–3, 5–4–3–2–1–5, 2–3–4–5–1–2

INTERVALLIC PATTERNS

Let's take a look at intervallic patterns (patterns distinguished by skipwise, rather than stepwise, motion). To develop great alternate picking technique, it's important to also be able to control string skips and jumps. Below, I have illustrated the possible intervals of the minor pentatonic. Again, everything is organized the same way: the Prime and Retrograde-Inversion will be shown in music and TAB, inversion and retrograde will be shown with scale tone formulas and pattern numbers.

Ex. 32A Track 53
Prime Pattern: 1–3, 2–4, 3–5, 4–1

Ex. 32B Track 54
Retrograde-Inversion Pattern: 2–5, 1–4, 5–3, 4–2

Ex. 32C
Inversion (Descending from Top String) Pattern: 5–2, 4–1, 3–5, 2–4
Scale Degrees: ♭7–♭3, 5–1, 4–♭7, ♭3–5, etc.

Ex. 32D
Retrograde (Ascending from Bottom String) Pattern: 3–1, 4–2, 5–3, 1–4
Scale Degrees: 4–1, 5–♭3, ♭7–4, 1–5, etc.

Ex. 33A Track 55
Prime (Ascending 4ths, Descending 4ths):
1–3, 4–2, 3–5, 1–4, etc.

Ex. 33B Track 56
Retrograde-Inversion (Descending 4ths, Ascending 4ths):
2–5, 4–1, 5–3, 2–4, etc.

Ex. 33C
Inversion (Descending from Top String) Pattern: 5–2, 1–4, 3–5, 4–2
Scale Degrees: ♭7–♭3, 1–5, 4–♭7, 5–♭3, etc.

Ex. 33D
Retrograde (Ascending from Bottom String) Pattern: 3–1, 2–4, 5–3, 4–1
Scale Degrees: 4–1, ♭3–5, ♭7–4, 5–1, etc.

Ex. 34A 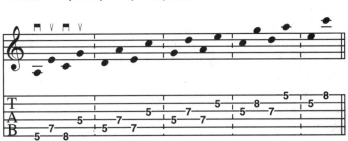 Track 57
Prime: 1–4, 2–5, 3–1, 4–2, etc.

Ex. 34B 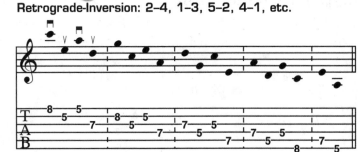 Track 58
Retrograde-Inversion: 2–4, 1–3, 5–2, 4–1, etc.

Ex. 34C
Inversion (Descending from Top String) Pattern: 4–2, 3–1, 2–5, 1–4
Scale Degrees: 5–♭3, 4–1, ♭3–♭7, 1–5, etc.

Ex. 34D
Retrograde (Ascending from Bottom String) Pattern: 4–1, 5–2, 1–3, 2–4
Scale Degrees: 5–1, 1–♭3, 1–4, ♭3–5, etc.

Ex. 35A  Track 59
Prime (Ascending 5ths, Descending 5ths):
1–4, 5–2, 3–1, 2–4, etc.

Ex. 35B  Track 60
Retrograde-Inversion (Descending 5ths, Ascending 5ths):
2–4, 3–1, 5–2, 1–4, etc.

Ex. 35C
Inversion (Descending from Top String) Pattern: 4–2, 1–3, 1–5, 4–1
Scale Degrees: 5–♭3, 5–4, ♭3–♭7, 5–1, etc.

Ex. 35D
Retrograde (Ascending from Bottom String) Pattern: 4–1, 2–5, 1–3, 4–2
Scale Degrees: 5–1, ♭3–♭7, 1–4, 5–♭3, etc.

Ex. 36A Track 61
Prime: 1–1, 2–2, 3–3, 4–4, etc.

Ex. 36B Track 62
Retrograde-Inversion: 2–2, 1–1, 5–5, 4–4, etc.

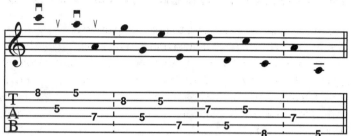

Ex. 36C
Inversion (Descending from Top String) Pattern: 2–2, 1–1, 5–5, 4–4
Scale Degrees: ♭3–♭3, 1–1, ♭7–♭7, 5–5, 4–4, etc.

Ex. 36D
Retrograde (Ascending from Bottom String) Pattern: 1–1, 2–2, 3–3, 4–4
Scale Degrees: 1–1, ♭3–♭3, 4–4, 5–5, ♭7–♭7

Ex. 37A
Prime (Ascending 8ths, Descending 8ths):
1–1, 2–2; 3–3, 4–4; etc.

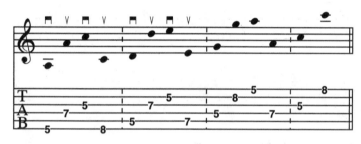

Ex. 37B
Retrograde-Inversion (Descending 8ths, Ascending 8ths):
2–2, 1–1; 5–5, 4–4; etc.

Ex. 37C
Inversion (Descending from Top String) Pattern: 2–2, 1–1, 5–5, 4–4
Scale Degrees: ♭3–♭3, 1–1; ♭7–♭7, 5–5; 4–4, ♭3–♭3; etc.

Ex. 37D
Retrograde (Ascending from Bottom String) Pattern: 1–1, 2–2, 3–3, 4–4
Scale Degrees: 1–1, ♭3–♭3; 4–4, 5–5; ♭7–♭7, 1–1; etc.

It's important to mention that there are many more combinations possible—for example, ascending 4ths and descending 5ths, etc.—but this is a great start to understanding the possibilities within the pentatonic or any other two-note-per-string scale. Obviously, you will need to apply these patterns to the other four positions of the pentatonic scale to cover the entire fretboard.

MELODIC SINGLE- AND TWO-STRING PATTERNS

The easiest and quickest way to get your picking skills up and running is by practicing small scale fragments and patterns that are repetitive and can be easily moved horizontally on the string and fretboard. Below, you will find a collection of patterns that are all essential melodic ideas that can be used in solos or melodies. Practice these patterns slowly within a chosen key, and then add the metronome to your practice routine. Stay in a single position at first with these exercises, but when you feel more comfortable in your guitar motor skills and music key knowledge, you can eventually play them from the 1st fret to the last fret of your guitar, eventually covering all six strings. If you are a seven- or eight-string player, these patterns will apply to all the other strings on your guitar as well.

SINGLE-STRING PATTERNS

Let's begin with single-string patterns. You can practice these elements either chromatically up and down the string, or you can adjust them to fit a particular key. Additionally, these examples are noted with a particular rhythm but they should also be played with other rhythms. For example, a triplet element can be interpreted as a sextuplet idea or as an even-more daring eighth- or 16th-note element. Of course, the same goes for examples that are notated as eighth- or 16th-note patterns.

Single-String Three-Note Patterns

Single-String Four-Note Patterns
Let's check out some four-note patterns that can be played as eighth notes or 16th notes.

Single-String Quintuplet and Septuplet Patterns

Here are some ideas that can be played as quintuplets or septuplets

TWO-STRING PATTERNS

Let's do some more complicated patterns. The following two-string patterns will help you with your pick coordination across strings and also prepare you for longer sequences that ascend and descend across strings in the following chapter. It's always better to practice complex movements in small segments rather than working through a long sequence. It's like eating a pizza. You wouldn't roll up a whole pizza and gobble it down, would you? Slice by slice is a better way to enjoy it!

Two-String Three- and Six-Note Patterns

Let's begin with triplet and sextuplet patterns.

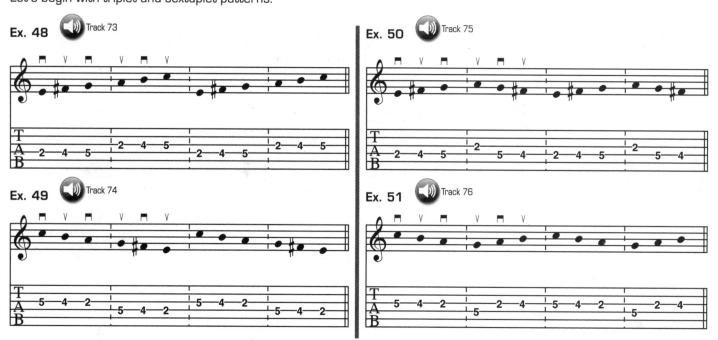

Let's try some busier patterns.

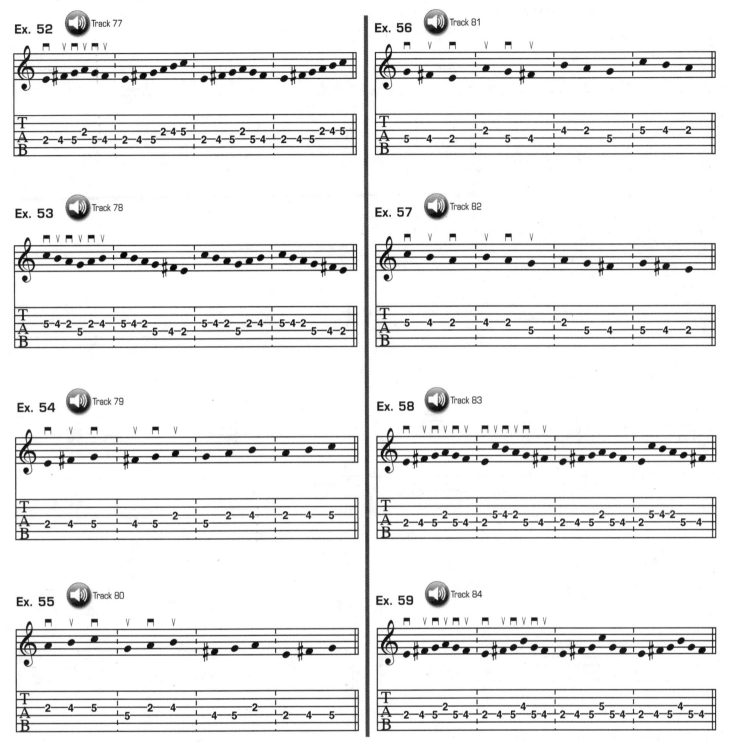

Two-String Four-Note Patterns

Let's continue with some patterns that could be played as eighth or 16th notes.

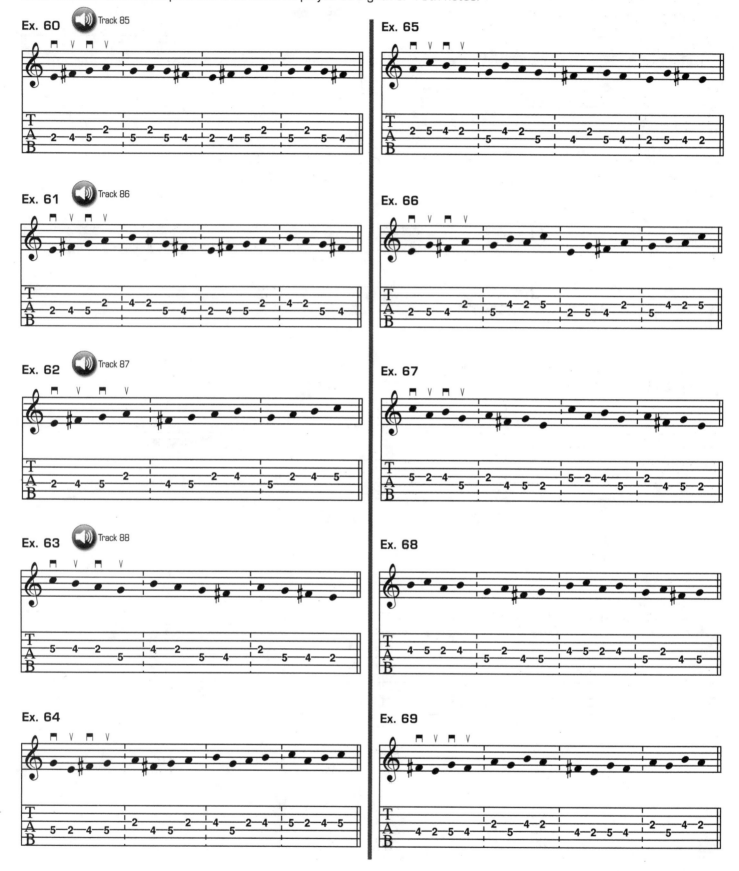

Two-String Five-Note Patterns
How about a few patterns of five?

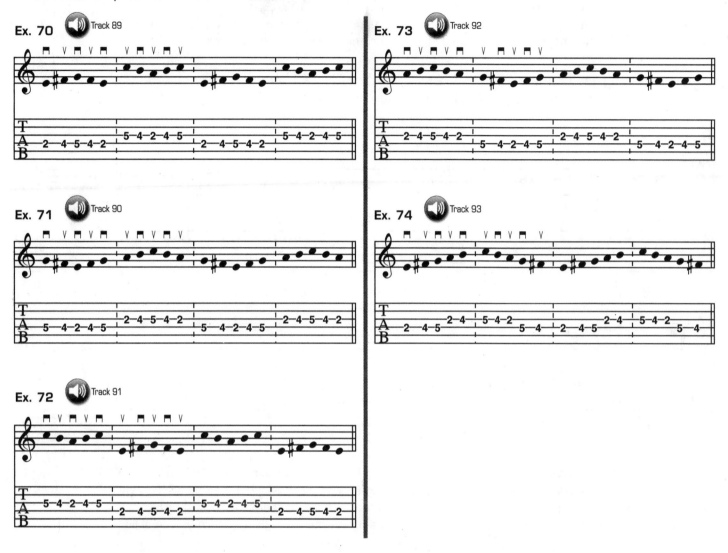

The above patterns are essential melodic ideas and movements. They are used in all musical forms, from classical music to death metal. I encourage you to go out and pick up some music scores from composers or bands that you like, and research their melodic patterns and elements. You will be surprised to find how much of the melodic material we use and play today has been around for centuries. Perhaps you will come across some new patterns and can add them to your playing, allowing you to explore new melodic grounds on the guitar!

Apply these patterns to all strings, string pairs, and all 12 keys. Practice one or two different patterns per day. Keep rotating these exercises to cover all of the patterns. This will work great to build up your technique as well as develop your melodic or solo playing.

CREATING A ROADMAP ON THE FRETBOARD

Practicing these melodic fragments in position is a great way to get your chops going. However, you can gain much more knowledge and skill if you organize your practice wisely. For instance, you can start by taking any of these patterns and play them up and down chromatically on one or two strings.

Sequencing a Three-Note Pattern on One String

In this exercise, a pattern outlining a minor 3rd is sequenced up the 3rd string chromatically.

Ex. 75 🔊 Track 94

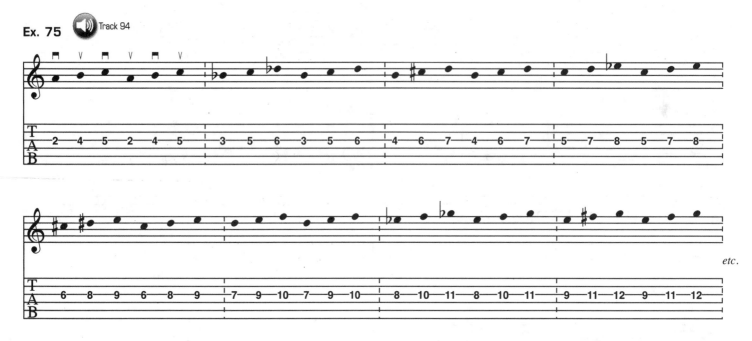

The next step is to connect the dots and place the pattern you are practicing in the context of a key. The exercise below shows you the previous pattern, but in the key of A Minor/C Major. Since we are taking the pattern through a key, playing a diatonic instead of chromatic sequence, sometimes we'll trace a minor 3rd and sometimes a major 3rd, though it is always a three-note ascending pattern on one string.

Ex. 76 🔊 Track 95

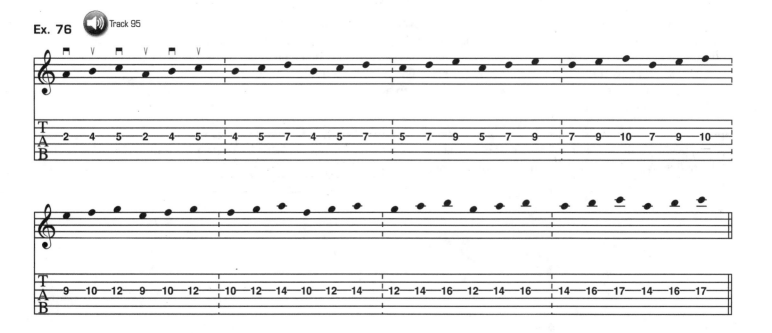

Continue to play the patterns horizontally (along a single string) on the guitar. When you run out of space, cross over to a higher, or lower, string and continue with the patterns within a key.

MOVING ACROSS THE GUITAR WITH A THREE-NOTE-PER-STRING SCALE

Let's take a closer look at possible melodic scale sequences from a standard three-note-per-string scale. Below is a diagram that illustrates the seven positions of the C Major scale. Even though, the names given to the positions are based on their modal names, these scale positions have nothing to do with the modes. It's about labeling the scale positions based on their relative starting point, and it's simply easier calling out an F Lydian scale rather than calling it the C Major scale from the 4th position or note. If you don't know the C Major three-note-per-string scale and its positions, you should learn and memorize them, as they are essential for building up technique and speed. The seven notes of the C Major scale are: C, D, E, F, G, A, and B, and the scale tone formula is: 1, 2, 3, 4, 5, 6, and 7.

Three-Note-per-String Scale Diagrams in C Major

Lydian

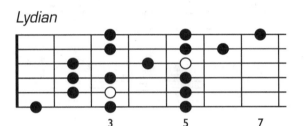

Mixolydian

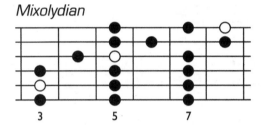

Aeolian (Minor)

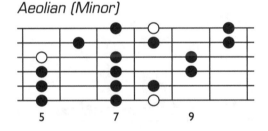

Locrian

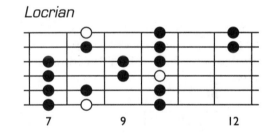

Ionian (Major)

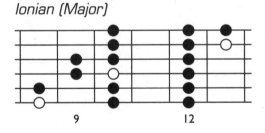

Dorian

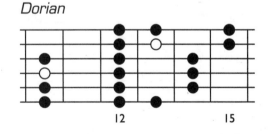

Phrygian

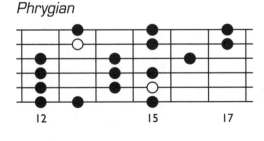

THREE- AND FOUR-NOTE PATTERNS

The following sequences display the basic three- and four-note patterns that are very common on the guitar. They will be a great asset to your playing and also add to your melodic vocabulary. Study these patterns slowly, and don't forget to use a metronome. Additionally, practice these ideas with all positions of the three-note-per-string scale as well.

Three-Note Patterns

Let's start out with three-note group sequences.

Ex. 77A Track 96
Prime Pattern: 1–2–3, 2–3–4, 3–4–5, 4–5–6, etc.

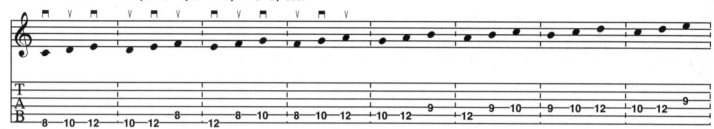

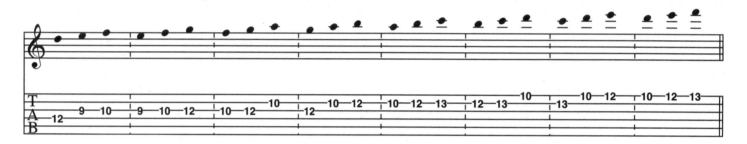

Ex. 77B Track 97
Retrograde-Inversion Pattern: 4–3–2, 3–2–1, 2–1–7, 1–7–6, etc.

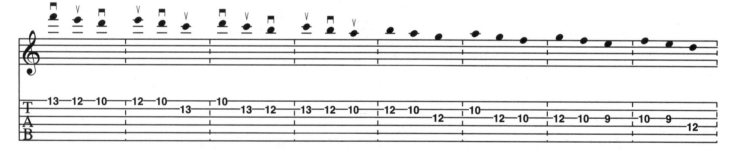

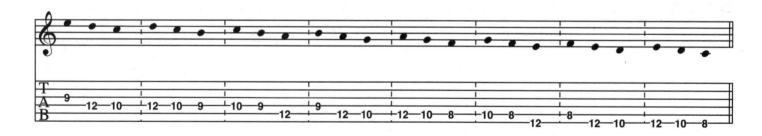

Develop the permutation using these formulas:

Ex. 77C
Inversion (Descending from Top String): 2–3–4, 1–2–3, 7–1–2, 6–7–1

Ex. 77D
Retrograde (Ascending from Bottom String): 3–2–1, 4–3–2, 5–4–3, 6–5–4

Let's combine the ascending and descending sequences!

Ex. 78A 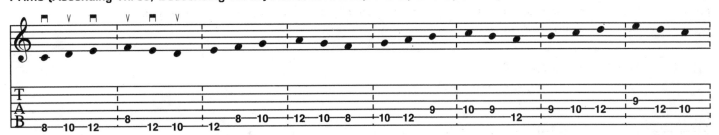 Track 98
Prime (Ascending Three, Descending Three) Pattern: 1–2–3, 4–3–2, 3–4–5, 6–5–4, etc.

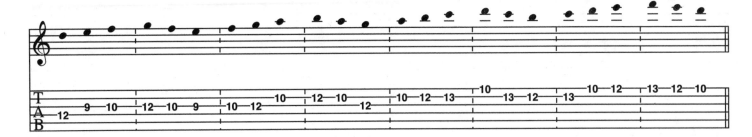

Ex. 78B 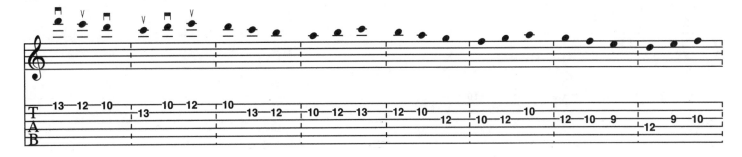 Track 99
Retrograde-Inversion (Descending Three, Ascending Three) Pattern: 4–3–2, 1–2–3, 2–1–7, 6–7–1, etc.

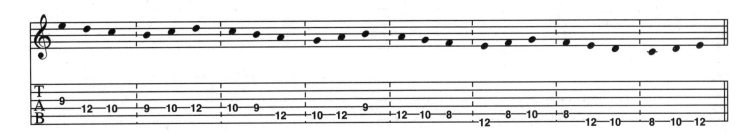

Ex. 78C
Inversion (Descending from Top String): 2–3–4, 3–2–1, 7–1–2, 1–7–6

Ex. 78D
Retrograde (Ascending from Bottom String): 3–2–1, 2–3–4, 5–4–3, 4–5–6

The following two exercises show how you can create three-note patterns from one note to the next and then return to the first note as applied to the C Major scale.

Ex. 79A 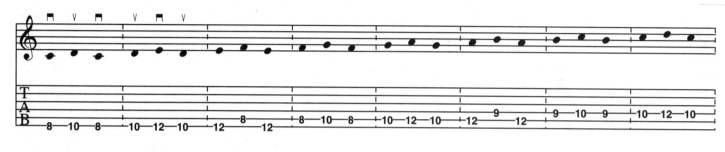 Track 100
Prime Pattern: 1–2–1, 2–3–2, 3–4–3, 4–5–4, etc.

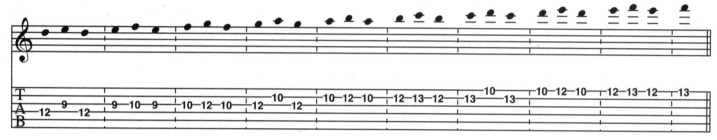

Ex. 79B Track 101
Retrograde-Inversion Pattern: 4–3–4, 3–2–3, 2–1–2, 1–7–1, etc.

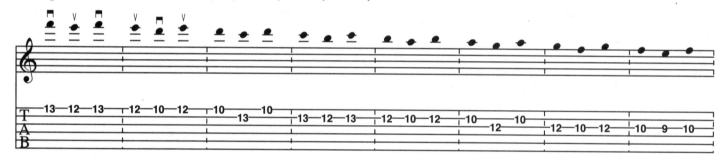

Here's the formula for the remaining sequences:

Ex. 79C
Inversion (Descending from Top String): 3–4–3, 2–3–2, 1–2–1, 7–1–7

Ex. 79D
Retrograde (Ascending from Bottom String): 2–1–2, 3–2–3, 4–3–4, 5–4–5

Try to develop more combinations and variations based on the idea of inserting other scale tones at the beginning of a three-note pattern.

Four-Note Patterns

The following sequences are based on groups of four notes. Let's begin with one of the most common scale sequences in music: ascending sequences of four notes.

Ex. 80A Track 102
Prime Pattern: 1–2–3–4, 2–3–4–5, 3–4–5–6, 4–5–6–7, etc.

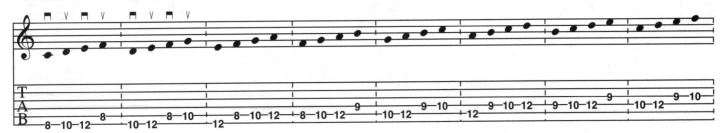

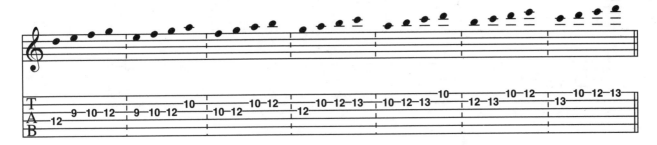

Ex. 80B Track 103
Retrograde-Inversion Pattern: 4–3–2–1, 3–2–1–7, 2–1–7–6, 1–7–6–5, etc.

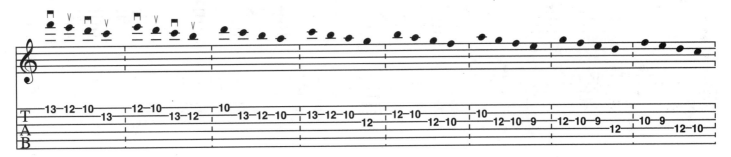

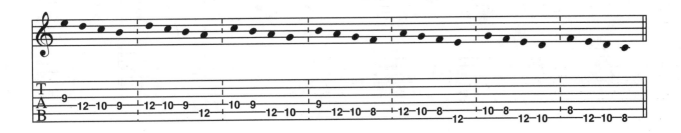

All right, now it's up to you to develop the permutations for this movement.

Ex. 80C
Inversion (Descending from Top String): 1–2–3–4, 7–1–2–3, 6–7–1–2, 5–6–7–1

Ex. 80D
Retrograde (Ascending from Bottom String): 4–3–2–1, 5–4–3–2, 6–5–4–3, 7–6–5–4

The next set of sequences are combinations of ascending and descending groups of four.

Ex. 81A  Track 104

Prime (Ascending Four, Descending Four) Pattern: 1–2–3–4, 5–4–3–2, 3–4–5–6, 7–6–5–4, etc.

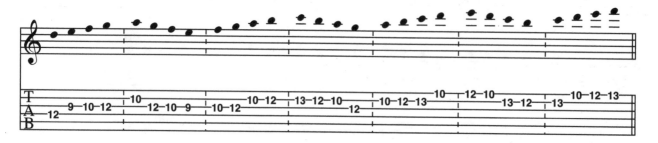

Ex. 81B Track 105

Retrograde-Inversion (Descending Four, Ascending Four) Pattern: 4–3–2–1, 7–1–2–3, 2–1–7–6, 5–6–7–1

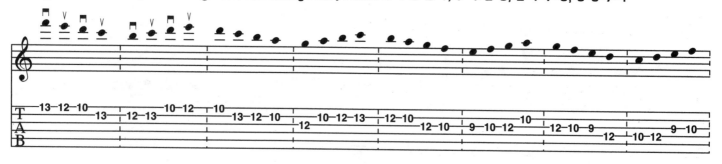

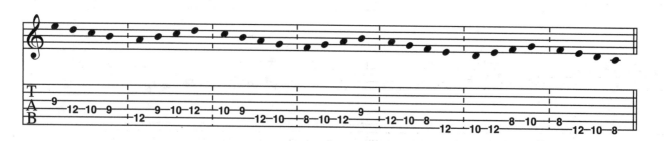

Ex. 81C

Inversion (Descending from Top String): 1–2–3–4, 3–2–1–7, 6–7–1–2, 1–7–6–5

Ex. 81D

Retrograde (Ascending from Bottom String): 4–3–2–1, 2–3–4–5, 6–5–4–3, 4–5–6–7

Let's take a look at a variation with a note displacement. Try to develop more ideas by either adding a note to the beginning of sequences or by simply offsetting the rhythm by a 16th note. You'll be amazed how many different new melodic patterns you can develop.

Ex. 82A
Prime Pattern: 3–1–2–3, 4–2–3–4, 5–3–4–5, 6–4–5–6, etc.

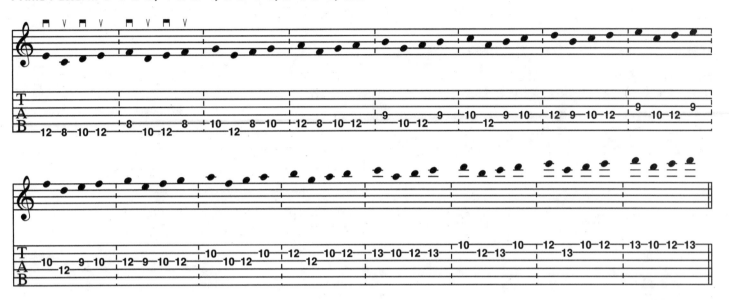

Ex. 82B
Retrograde-Inversion Pattern: 2–4–3–2, 1–3–2–1, 7–2–1–7, 6–1–7–6, etc.

Ex. 82C
Inversion (Descending from Top String): 4–2–3–4, 3–1–2–3, 2–7–1–2, 1–6–7–1

Ex. 82D
Retrograde (Ascending from Bottom String): 1–3–2–1, 2–4–3–2, 3–5–4–3, 4–6–5–4

FIVE- AND SIX-NOTE PATTERNS

The sequences and their permutations that we just discussed are very common musical ideas and movements. You can find them in all genres of music, played by many different instruments. Let's examine different note groupings next. The following sequences deal with groupings of five and six, and their possible combinations.

Five-Note Patterns

Let's take a look at this ascending five-note sequence.

Ex. 83A  Track 106
Prime Pattern: 1–2–3–4–5, 2–3–4–5–6, 3–4–5–6–7, 4–5–6–7–1, etc.

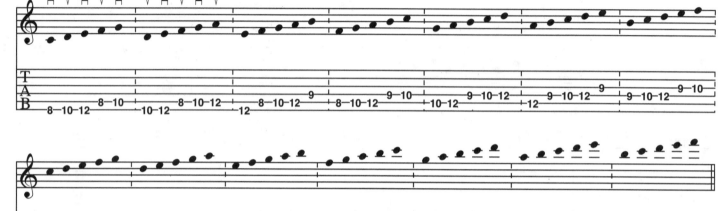

Since we are using a three-note-per-string scale, it will be more challenging to develop a good fingering for the groups of five notes. But, once you memorize the pattern and lock into the rhythm, it will flow very well, resulting in a very interesting sound.

Let's start by trying this:

Ex. 83B  Track 107
Retrograde-Inversion Pattern: 4–3–2–1–7, 3–2–1–7–6, 2–1–7–6–5, 1–7–6–5–4, etc.

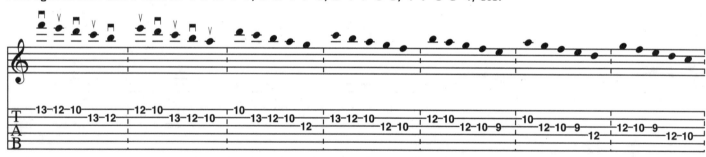

Ex. 83C
Inversion (Descending from Top String): 7–1–2–3–4, 6–7–1–2–3, 5–6–7–1–2, 4–5–6–7–1

Ex. 83D
Retrograde (Ascending from Bottom String): 5–4–3–2–1, 6–5–4–3–2, 7–6–5–4–3, 1–7–6–5–4

Let's combine the movements.

Ex. 84A Track 108
Prime (Ascending Five, Descending Five) Pattern: 1–2–3–4–5, 6–5–4–3–2; 3–4–5–6–7, 1–7–6–5–4; etc.

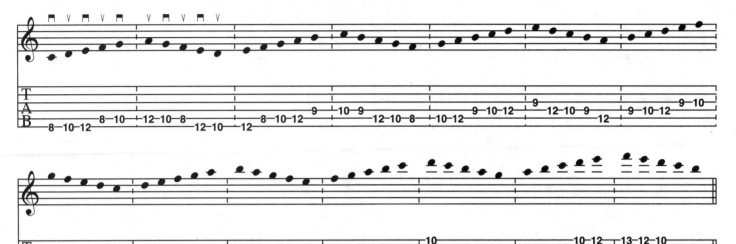

Ex. 84B Track 109
Retrograde-Inversion (Descending Five, Ascending Five) Pattern: 4–3–2–1–7, 6–7–1–2–3; 2–1–7–6–5, 4–5–6–7–1; etc.

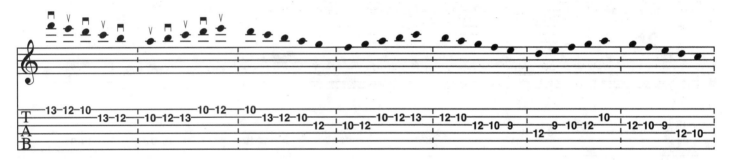

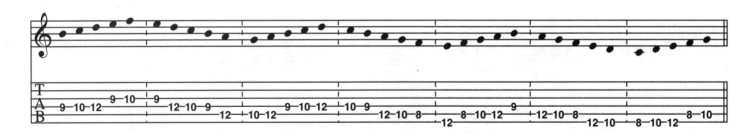

Ex. 84C
Inversion (Descending from Top String): 7–1–2–3–4, 3–2–1–7–6; 5–6–7–1–2, 1–7–6–5–4; etc.

Ex. 84D
Retrograde (Ascending from Bottom String): 5–4–3–2–1, 2–3–4–5–6; 7–6–5–4–3, 4–5–6–7–1; etc.

Six-Note Patterns

Are you ready for some more unusual patterns? Let's extend it to six-note groupings.

Ex. 85A 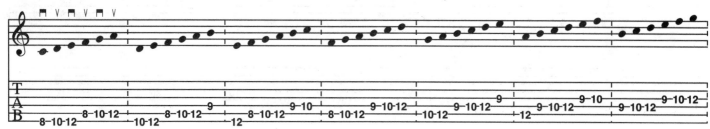 Track 110

Prime Pattern: 1–2–3–4–5–6, 2–3–4–5–6–7, 3–4–5–6–7–1, 4–5–6–7–1–2, etc.

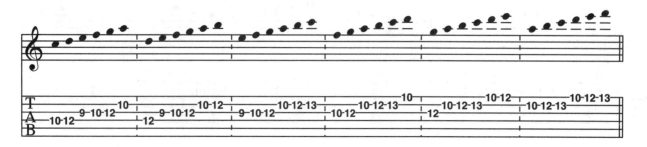

Ex. 85B Track 111

Retrograde-Inversion Pattern: 4–3–2–1–7–6, 3–2–1–7–6–5, 2–1–7–6–5–4, 1–7–6–5–4–3, etc.

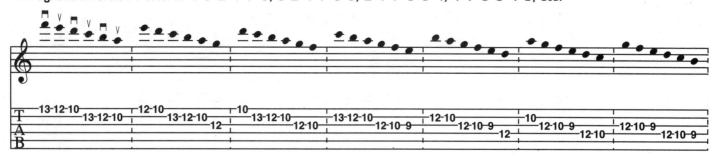

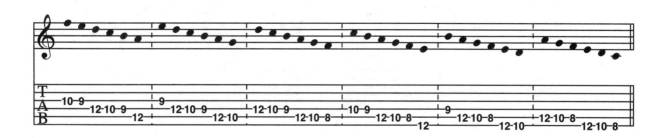

As mentioned, the hardest part here may be in developing good fingerings to play these note groupings fluently. Take your time, and most importantly, play it slowly and utilize all scale positions.

Ex. 85C

Inversion (Descending from Top String): 6–7–1–2–3–4, 5–6–7–1–2–3, 4–5–6–7–1–2, 3–4–5–6–7–1

Ex. 85D

Retrograde (Ascending from Bottom String): 6–5–4–3–2–1, 7–6–5–4–3–2, 1–7–6–5–4–3, 2–1–7–6–5–4

It's time to combine the groupings of six. Check these out:

Ex. 86A 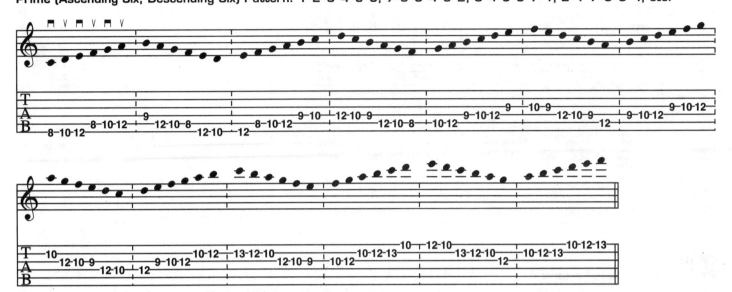 Track 112
Prime (Ascending Six, Descending Six) Pattern: 1–2–3–4–5–6, 7–6–5–4–3–2; 3–4–5–6–7–1, 2–1–7–6–5–4; etc.

Ex. 86B Track 113
Retrograde-Inversion (Descending Six, Ascending Six): 4–3–2–1–7–6, 5–6–7–1–2–3; 2–1–7–6–5–4, 3–4–5–6–7–1; etc.

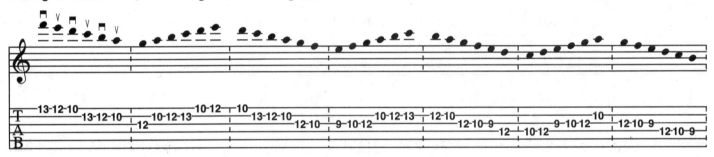

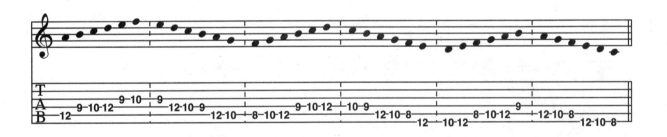

Ex. 86C
Inversion (Descending from Top String): 6–7–1–2–3–4, 3–2–1–7–6–5, 4–5–6–7–1–2, 1–7–6–5–4–3

Ex. 86D
Retrograde (Ascending from Bottom String): 6–5–4–3–2–1, 2–3–4–5–6–7, 1–7–6–5–4–3, 4–5–6–7–1–2

Here are a few patterns in six. These ideas are more guitar-player friendly but have a great sound and flow to them. Try to develop a few more. There's no limit to how you can set up your sequences.

Ex. 87A Track 114
Prime Pattern: 1-2-3-4-5-6, 4-5-6-7-1-2, 7-1-2-3-4-5, 3-4-5-6-7-1, etc.

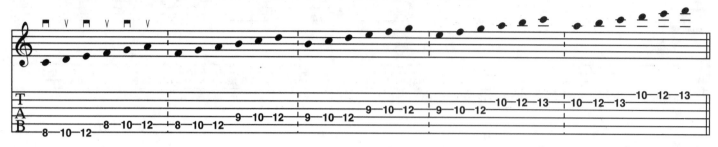

Ex. 87B Track 115
Retrograde-Inversion Pattern: 4-3-2-1-7-6, 1-7-6-5-4-3, 5-4-3-2-1-7, 2-1-7-6-5-4, etc.

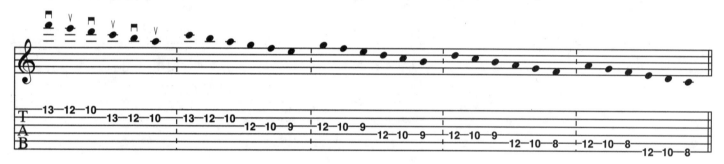

Try these next:

Ex. 87C
Inversion (Descending from Top String): 2-3-4-6-7-1, 6-7-1-3-4-5, 3-4-5-7-1-2, 7-1-2-4-5-6

Ex. 87D
Retrograde (Ascending from Bottom String): 3-2-1-6-5-4, 6-5-4-2-1-7, 2-1-7-5-4-3, 5-4-3-1-7-6

How about these challenging movements?

Ex. 88A
Prime (Ascending Six, Descending Six) Pattern: 1–2–3–4–5–6, 2–1–7–6–5–4, 7–1–2–3–4–5, 1–7–6–5–4–3, etc.

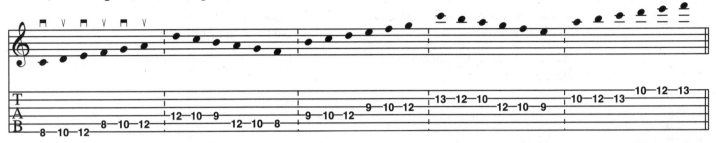

Ex. 88B
Retrograde-Inversion (Descending Six, Ascending Six) Pattern: 4–3–2–1–7–6, 3–4–5–6–7–1,
5–4–3–2–1–7, 4–5–6–7–1–2, etc.

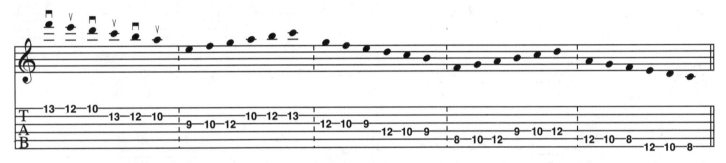

Ex. 88C
Inversion (Descending from Top String): 6–7–1–2–3–4, 1–7–6–5–4–3, 7–1–2–3–4–5, 2–1–7–6–5–4, 1–2–3–4–5–6

Ex. 88D
Retrograde (Ascending from Bottom String): 6–5–4–3–2–1, 4–5–6–7–1–2, 5–4–3–2–1–7, 3–4–5–6–7–1, 4–3–2–1–7–6

INTERVALS

To further develop your picking technique, speed, and accuracy, try the advanced patterns in this chapter. They are based on intervals such as 2nds, 3rds, 4ths, 5ths, 6ths, 7ths, and octaves. Try these very slowly, and understand the developing patterns and sounds, before you set a metronome to it. Additionally, try to develop all the permutations and combinations just as we have up till now.

All these exercises are played with strict alternate picking. Use all positions of the three-note-per-string scale to practice these ideas.

2NDS

Ex. 89A
Prime

 Track 116

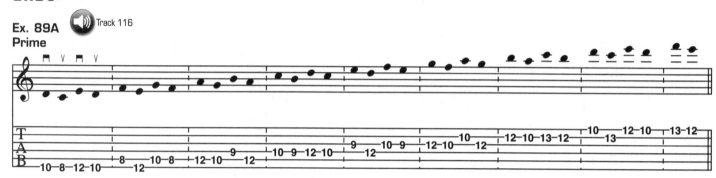

Ex. 89B
Retrograde-Inversion

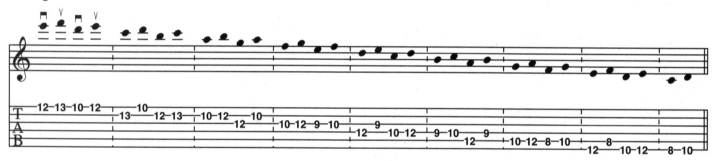

3RDS

Ex. 90A
Prime

 Track 117

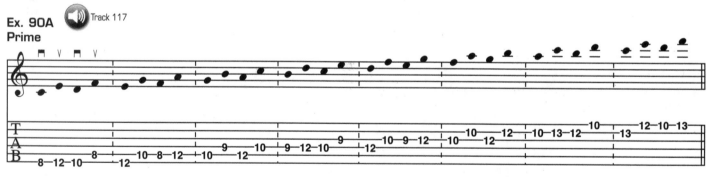

Ex. 90B
Retrograde-Inversion

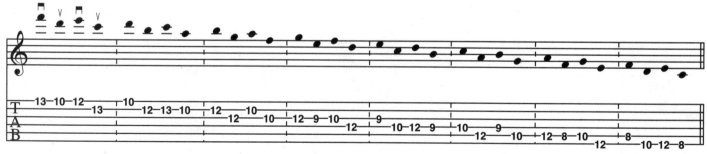

Ex. 91A
Prime

Ex. 91B
Retrograde-Inversion

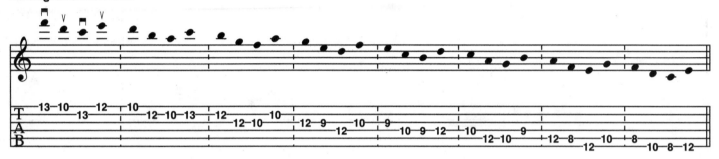

4THS

Ex. 92A
 Track 118
Prime

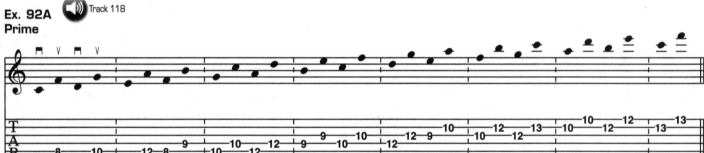

Ex. 92B
Retrograde-Inversion

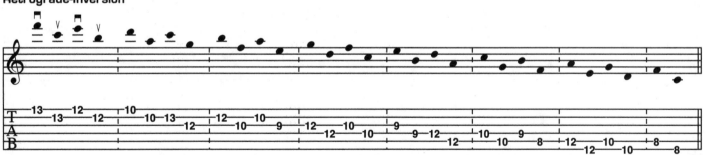

Ex. 93A
Prime

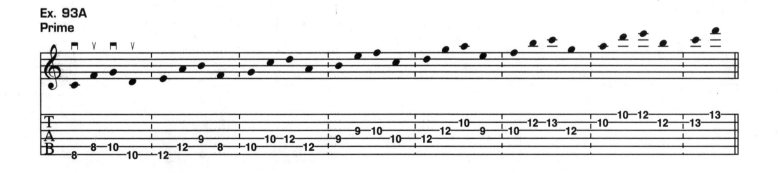

Ex. 93B
Retrograde-Inversion

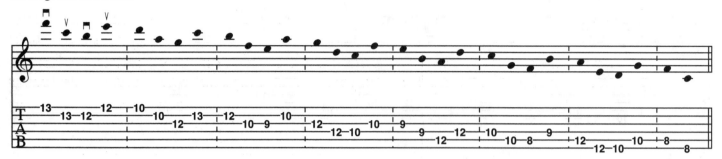

5THS

Ex. 94A
Prime Track 119

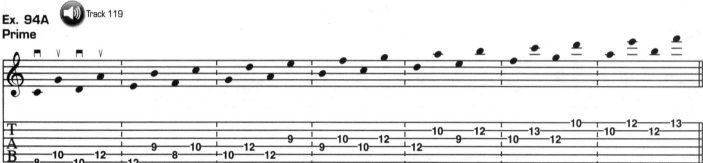

Ex. 94B
Retrograde-Inversion

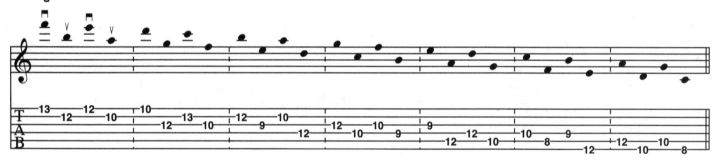

Ex. 95A
Prime

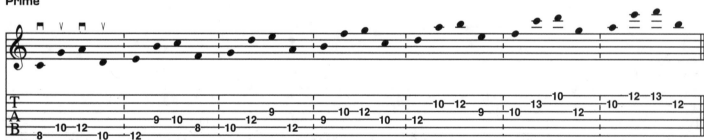

Ex. 95B
Retrograde-Inversion

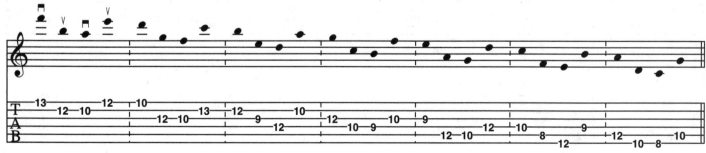

6THS

Ex. 96A
Prime

Track 120

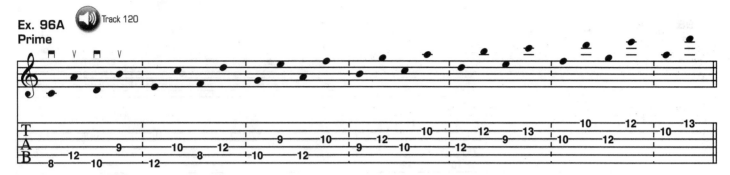

Ex. 96B
Retrograde-Inversion

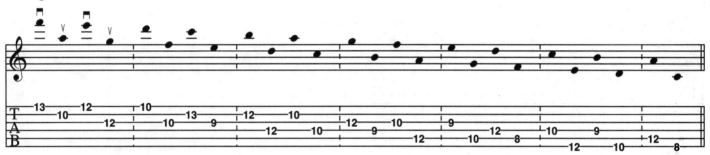

Ex. 97A
Prime

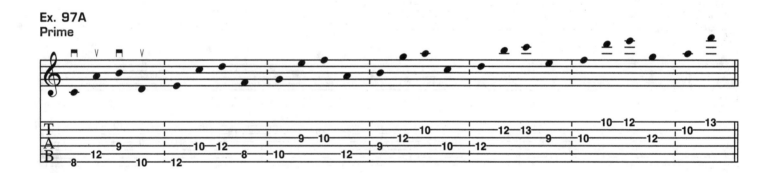

Ex. 97B
Retrograde-Inversion

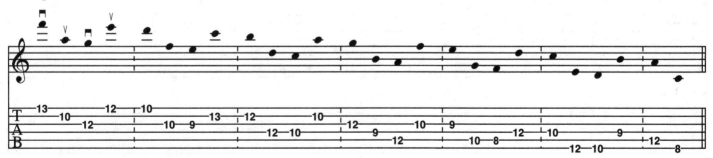

7THS

Ex. 98A  Track 121
Prime

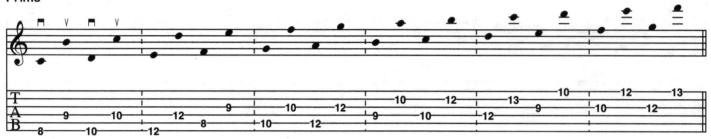

Ex. 98B Retrograde-Inversion

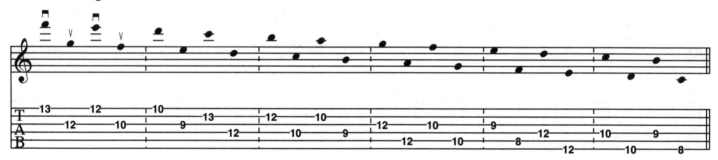

Ex. 99A Prime

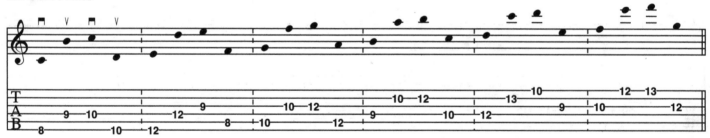

Ex. 99B Retrograde-Inversion

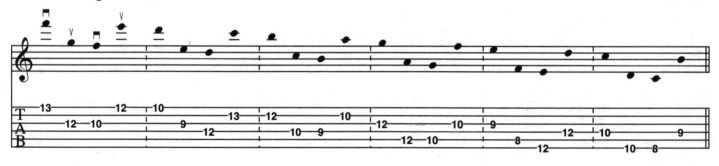

OCTAVES

Ex. 100A 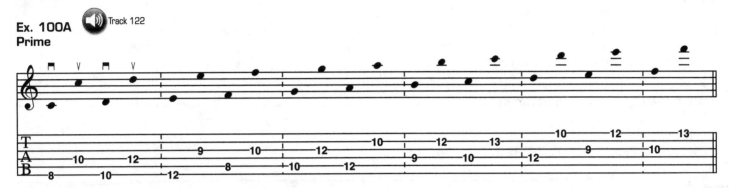 Track 122
Prime

Ex. 100B Retrograde-Inversion

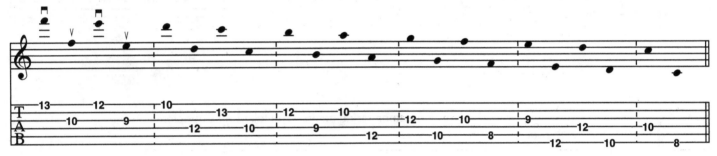

Ex. 101A Prime

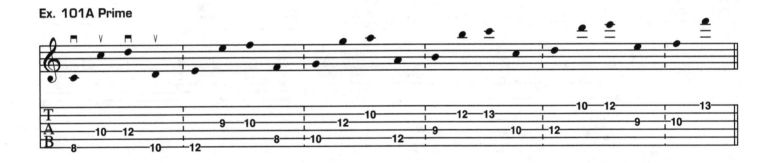

Ex. 101B Retrograde-Inversion

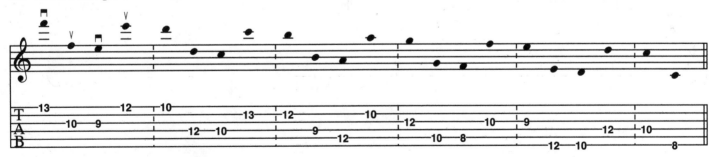

INTERVALLIC LICKS IN C MAJOR

Learning and applying all these intervallic patterns to your playing can lead to some very interesting lines, especially when you combine different intervallic movements. The execises below illustrate intervallic licks with the C Major Scale. Try your own combination of intervals and different scale positions. These ideas will certainly give you a great picking and coordination workout.

Intervallic Combinations

Ex. 102 Track 123
Pattern: 1–3–2–5, 3–5–4–7, 5–7–6–2, 7–2–1–4, etc.

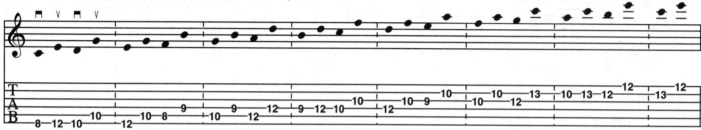

Now, take this idea and move it to the other three-note-per-string scales. The following examples feature a combination of ascending 5ths and descending 6ths.

Ex. 103 Track 124
Pattern: 1–5–7–2, 3–7–1–3, 4–1–2–4, 5–2–3–5, etc.

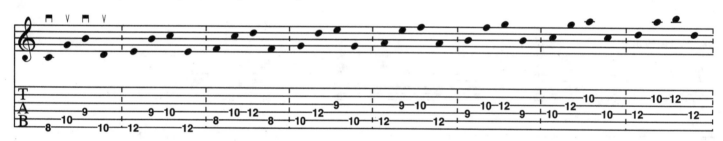

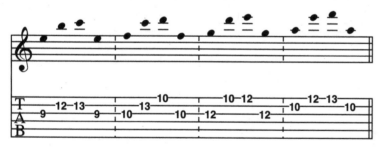

HARMONIC AND MELODIC MINOR SCALE FORMS

Practice the previous exercises with the harmonic and melodic minor scales, as well as other scales. This will take time and patience, but no one ever said the guitar was an easy thing! Always think of ways to improve your playing and knowledge. There are so many amazing concepts and great music out there. Following are scale forms you should memorize and apply to everything you have learned.

Harmonic Minor Scale Forms

Form 1

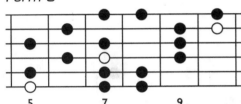

Form 2

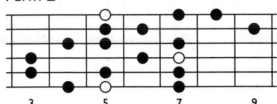

Form 3

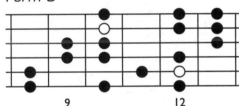

Form 4

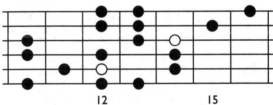

Form 5

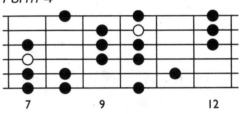

Form 6

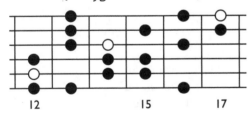

Form 7 (Phrygian Dominant)

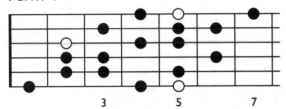

Melodic Minor Scale Forms

Locrian ♮2

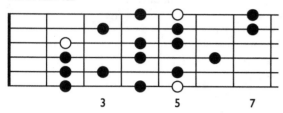

Altered Dominant

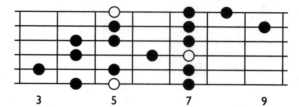

Melodic Minor

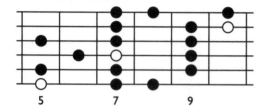

Dorian ♭2

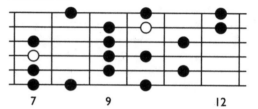

Lydian #5

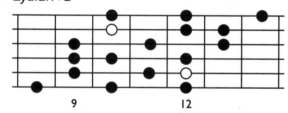

Lydian ♭7

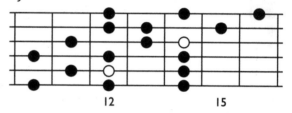

Mixolydian ♭6

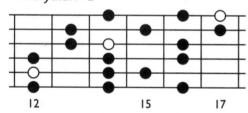

Practice Tip

You can view the harmonic and melodic minor scales as separate, new scales, but it helps to relate them to the natural minor scale. If you raise the 7th scale degree of a natural minor scale, it becomes a harmonic minor scale. If you raise the 6th degree of the harmonic minor scale, the scale turns into melodic minor. So, rather than simply learning and practicing the 14 total forms of the harmonic and melodic minor scales, try to identify the notes that need to change between those scales, which will help you get to know the scale and fretboard better. This will make learning and using these scales much more fun and natural.

GETTING INTO THE DETAILS

THE PENTATONIC SCALE

Now that we have covered various patterns and scale movements, it's time to take everything apart again and look at the things in a new way. Scales on the guitar are traditionally organized in a very clear way, through repetitive patterns or shapes. These patterns can be easily identified and then replicated octaves higher or lower to produce the same group of notes. Additionally, these patterns will also show you how all scales and their representative patterns are built.

The pentatonic scale and its different positions can be broken down to five easy shapes, or forms that can be combined in different ways to create various scale patterns..

Pentatonic Scale Form Fragments

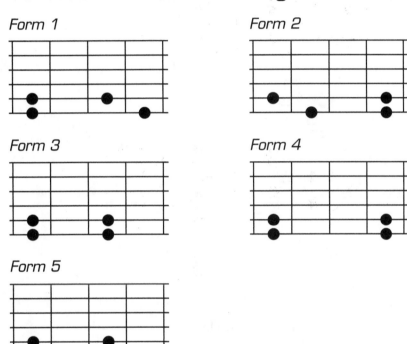

Form 1

Form 2

Form 3

Form 4

Form 5

These five pentatonic scale forms can be repeated on each octave of the form. Keep in mind that the shape will be distorted one fret to the right when you apply any shape to the G and B strings, as those strings are tuned a major 3rd apart—instead of the perfect 4th between the other strings. The example below shows you how form 5 repeats itself in different octaves across the fretboard.

Ex. 104 Track 125

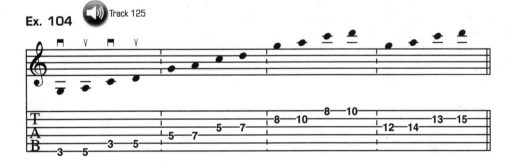

Instead of playing pentatonic scales vertically up and down, you can also combine all these forms on a string pair, like in the exercise below, to play the scale horizontally.

Ex. 105 Track 126

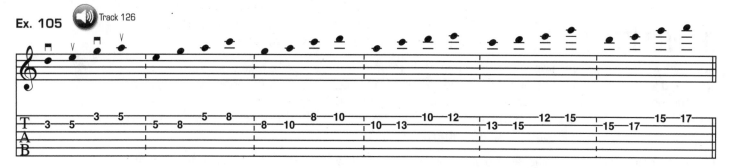

Let's look closer at all the forms of this scale to see how they overlap in each position. The example below shows you where the forms are when stacked on top of each other for the most commonly played scale, the A Minor Pentatonic.

Ex. 106 Track 127

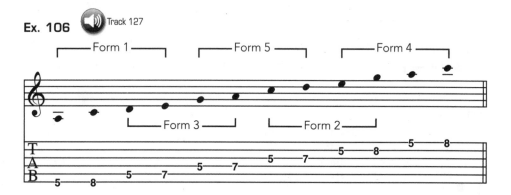

As you can see, these forms move in a particular way. Form 1 is followed by form 3, then form 5, then form 2, and finally form 4. You may notice that the forms in the scale will skip over its adjacent form—or, to look at it another way, most of the forms overlap by 4th intervals.

Now, you are probably wondering why this doesn't apply to forms 2 and 4. Form 2 and form 4 are not a 4th apart. Remember, the pentatonic scale is not built out of a series of whole and half steps, like a major scale, and doesn't have seven notes. This leaves only a limited number of intervallic possibilities. So, as it turns out, forms 2 and 4 are a major 3rd apart, instead of a 4th. Generally, the forms will always skip over its subsequent adjacent form when built vertically. Examine the other four remaining positions of the pentatonic scale to test this idea.

THE THREE-NOTE-PER-STRING SCALE

The way the guitar works can often be miraculous and sometimes confusing. The previously covered method of breaking everything down into shapes got us more clarity with the major scale and its workings, so now let's break the three-note-per-string scale down into its basic forms.

Three-Note-per-String Scale Forms

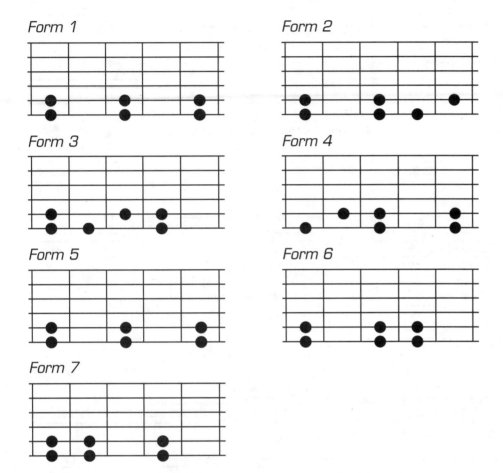

Form 1

Form 2

Form 3

Form 4

Form 5

Form 6

Form 7

Repeating a Three-Note-per-String Form from Octave to Octave

These basic seven forms can be simply moved from octave to octave, resulting in *hexatonic* scales.

Ex. 107 Track 128

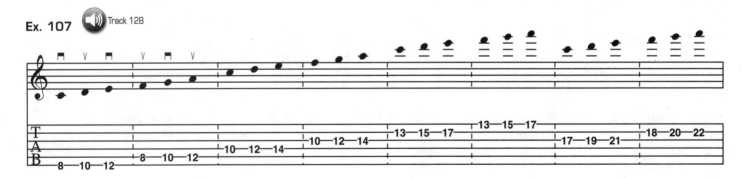

Try this idea of moving a form from octave to octave with the remaining six forms, starting from each respective position, meaning form 2 will start on the second pitch of a major scale and so forth.

All these forms can also be aligned on any string pair on the guitar. The following exercises illustrate this.

Ex. 108 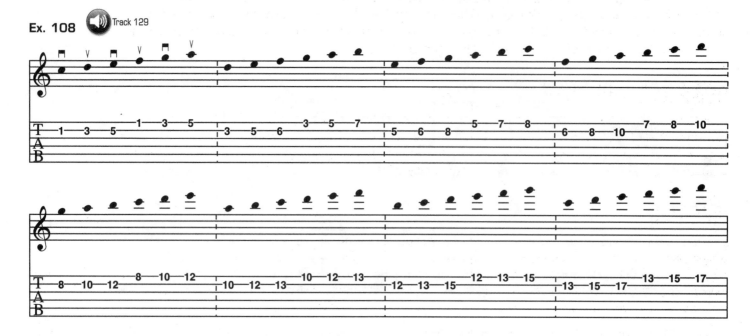 Track 129

Let's examine the major scale position. We will break this scale into its forms and then examine the details.

Ex. 109 Track 130

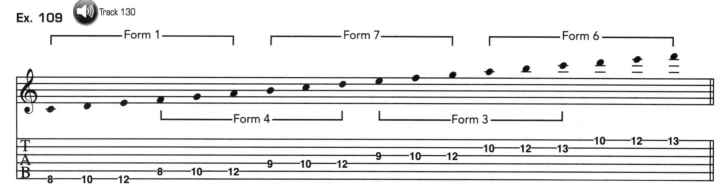

Beginning with form 1, the scale forms progress as follows: 1, 4, 7, 3, and 6. If you play a seven- or eight-string guitar, these patterns will continue in the same way. Knowing this, you can now learn and understand all your scales, no matter how many strings you play, by observing how the three-note-per-string forms combine to create them. Also, remember the forms will be distorted by one fret to the right on the G and B strings.

The Circle of 4ths
The major scale breaks down in the same interval structure as the pentatonic. The forms align in 4th intervals, and this intervallic structure is also coincidently known as the *circle of 4ths*, one of the most important concepts in music.

Starting from 1, the circle of 4ths is: 1, 4, 7, 3, 6, 2, 5, and 1. Think of this as its formula. All three-note-per-string scale structures are based on this principle. Analyze the remaining six scale positions of the major scale, as well as the harmonic minor and melodic minor scale, and you will see the underlying structures.

Practice Tip
Pick one of the single-string patterns, and play them through the various octaves with the five forms of the pentatonic scale or seven forms of the major scale. This is a great chop- and speed-building exercise, as you will need to recognize the different octave jumps quickly. And even though you may be tonally limited to either four or six notes, the result is a very impressive lick.

SPEED DEVELOPMENT AND ABSOLUTE PICK CONTROL

To develop great speed, control, and technique on the guitar, it is important to be aware of rhythm. All the patterns, sequences, and scales you have learned require rhythmic control and the ability to adjust, or change, rhythms and feels. Understanding a particular rhythm also means to have absolute control of the synchronization between the picking and fretting hands.

USING A METRONOME

Your best two friends for gaining absolute control of rhythm are the metronome and the rhythm pyramid. It is imperative that you always practice with a metronome and that you are very aware of rhythmic phrasing when playing licks and exercises. When you are not aware, you may find yourself losing control of your left- and right-hand coordination, even when playing within the context of music and a steady beat.

PRACTICE

In this chapter, we will examine strategies for practicing and gaining control of your fretboard. To start, always have a means to document your progress, as it is important to have a balanced and objective view on your progress. I usually write down my tempos and practice objectives for the day or week into a small journal. Your entries can be as detailed and elaborate, or as short, as you wish. The most important thing is that you know what and how you are working on your set goals and exercises.

Additionally, practice with clean, overdriven, and distorted guitar tones separately. You will find that isolating the individual guitar tones with the same exercises will present their own challenges and lead to better control, intonation, and feel.

USING THE RHYTHM PYRAMID

If you are not familiar with the rhythm pyramid, it's simply a way to organize and view rhythmic subdivisions. Firstly, try to clap rhythms before you play them on your guitar. Start by clapping the entire pyramid, from the top down and back. You may find that it is not so easy to play or clap all the rhythmic phrases correctly.

The Rhythm Pyramid Track 131

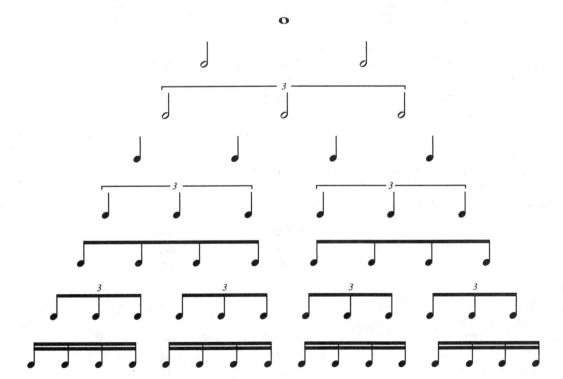

THE COORDINATION CHALLENGE

Now that you have practiced basic rhythms, let's take a closer look at simply playing a two-note- or three-note-per-string scale up and down the fretboard. The following exercises feature the A Minor Pentatonic scale played as eighth notes, eighth-note triplets, 16th notes, and sextuplets.

The difficult part here is to keep time and maintain synchronization, as the note distribution on the strings is not aligned with the rhythmic placement. Guitar players like the organization of their phrasing and note groups to be supported by the positions of notes on a string. However, in these exercises, we purposefuly avoid that. Set your metronome to a slow speed, and pay close attention to the rhythm and proper execution of technique.

A MINOR PENTATONIC COORDINATION EXERCISES

Eighth Notes

Ex. 110  Track 132

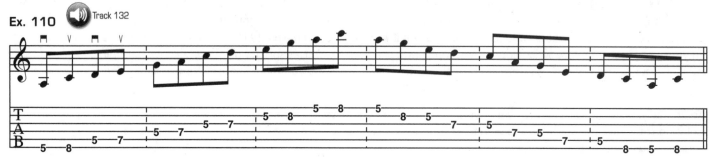

Eighth-Note Triplet

Ex. 111 Track 133

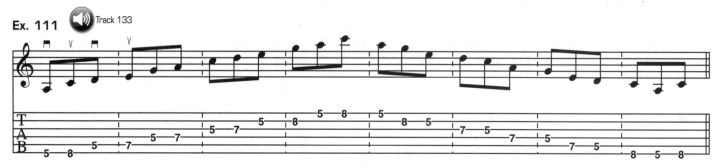

16th Notes

Ex. 112 Track 134

Sextuplets

Ex. 113 Track 135

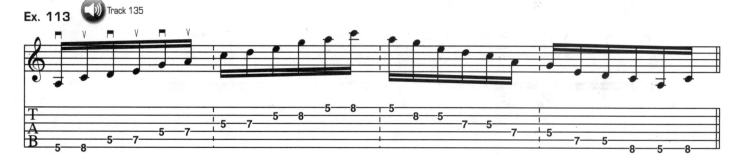

Try to play through the rhythms in the preceding exercises until your first note lands on beat 1 again. This might require some cycling and, depending on the tempo, could prove to be quite difficult. Now, try to do this with the other positions, so that your hands and rhythmic feel can really learn and memorize the various rhythms.

A MAJOR COORDINATION EXERCISES

The next set of exercises illustrates the same idea, only applied to the A Major three-note-per-string scale. Try it slowly and be patient, as these are difficult to play. But remember, these are just simple ascending and descending scales.

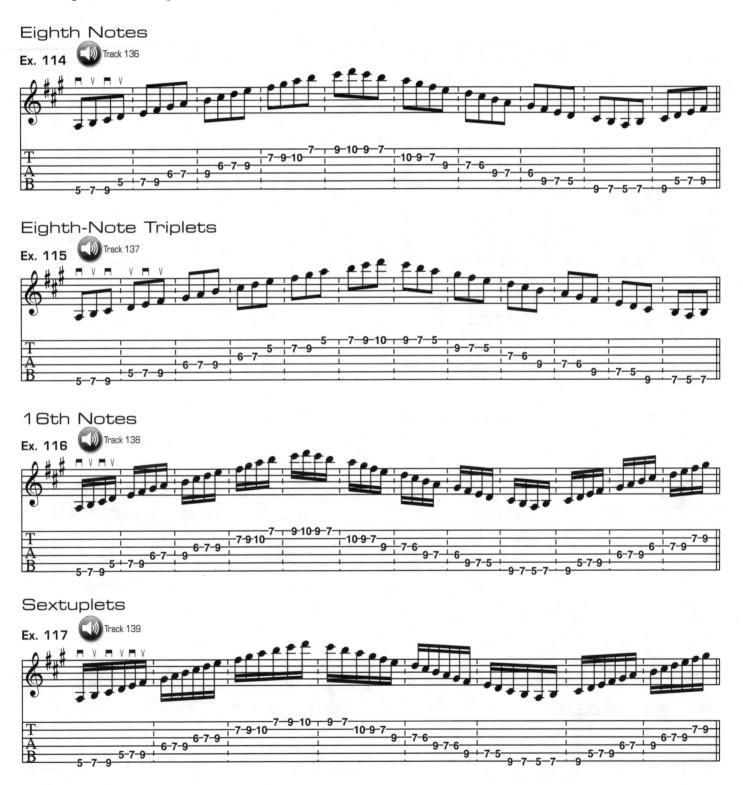

Eighth Notes

Ex. 114   Track 136

Eighth-Note Triplets

Ex. 115   Track 137

16th Notes

Ex. 116   Track 138

Sextuplets

Ex. 117   Track 139

Yes, these exercises are designed to challenge you, so don't give up! Keep practicing these ideas with all the other scales you know and play.

RHYTHM PYRAMID COORDINATION EXERCISES

The next exercise is also based on the rhythm pyramid. Here you will work your way though the different subdivisions with a small musical lick or phrase at a steady metronome setting.

Find your comfort tempo, then set the metronome lower than that since the subdivisions here will start from simple eighth notes and go all the way to 32nd notes. Even a basic tempo of 100 BPM can be quite fast and challenging. The goal here is to learn and feel the rhythms and be in control of your picking hand.

Eighth Notes and Eighth-Note Triplets
To start, let's try switching between an eighth-note and eighth-note-triplet feel.

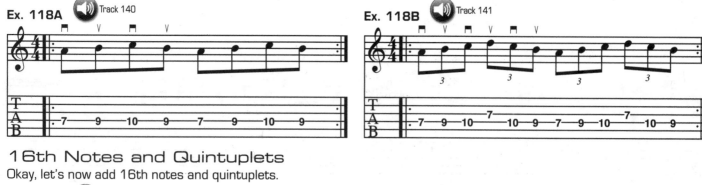

16th Notes and Quintuplets
Okay, let's now add 16th notes and quintuplets.

 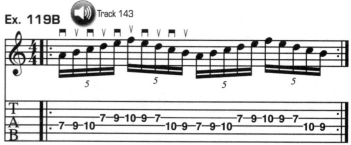

Try to go back and forth between the different rhythmic subdivisions as that will challenge you to have good pick control. Again, precision is more important than sheer speed here. As you gain rhythmic control, you will also affect your speed and general technique. Be patient and don't overextend yourself.

16th-Note Triplets and Septuplets
Now, let's kick it up a notch.

 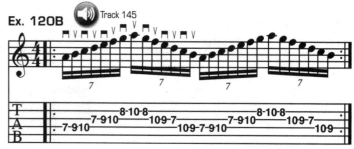

32nd Notes
And finally, here's the last subdivision

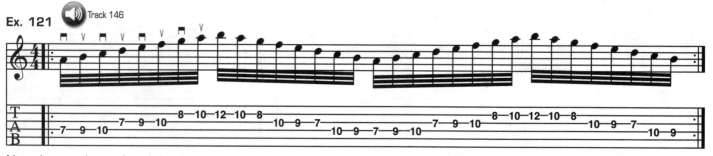

Now that you have played these exercises individually, it's time to play them back-to-back. Again, strive for accuracy rather than speed. This exercise will help your speed, precision, and pick control.

The next step is to move this phrase to other string combinations and also to extend these phrases.

BURST OR BUST

Another challenging way to practice your pick control and speed is the "burst" method. Here, you play a small musical fragment at a moderate tempo, then burst out and play it as fast as you can, and then slow it down again. This is a very popular technique and yields great results.

I like to incorporate the metronome into this idea by simply doubling up the rhythm of the original phrase. This means if the fragment is played as eighth notes, it will be played as 16th notes. Or, if it is played as eighth-note triplets, then it will be played as sextuplets. This method will help with placing musical phrases in the direct context of music. Again, focus on pick control and rhythmic understanding to yield results in speed and accuracy.

Burst Exercises

Practice all the exercises from the previous chapter with these rhythmic ideas.

MORE RHYTHMIC VARIATIONS

Ever notice how certain rhythms tend to set the pattern for scale movements? For example, ascending scale patterns in three will often be played as triplets. Of course, that makes perfect sense, but how about we juxtapose another rhythm over the pattern, let's say a 16th-note feel. That would look like this:

Ascending Scale Pattern in Triplets

Ex. 126 Track 151

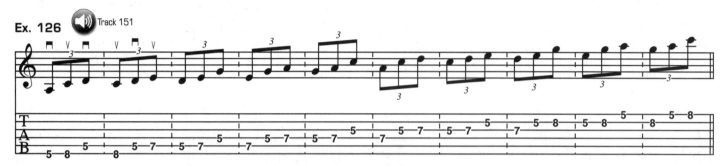

The Same Ascending Scale Pattern in 16th Notes

Ex. 127 Track 152

Four-Note Ascending Sequence

What happens if we take a four-note ascending sequence, like this:

Ex. 128 Track 153

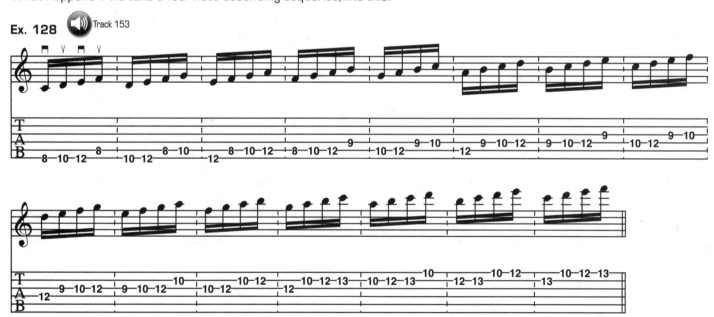

The Same Four-Note Ascending Sequence in Triplets
And apply a different rhythmic feel, like triplets? It turns into this:

Ex. 129 Track 154

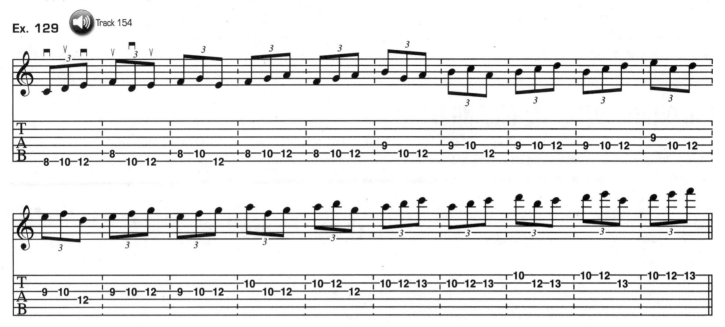

The Same Four-Note Ascending Sequence in Sextuplets
Now, let's double the feel and change it to sextuplets!

Ex. 130 Track 155

As you can see, you can turn a simple exercise into something fresh and unexpected with this concept. And at the same time, it will allow you to work on your speed, coordination, and musicianship.

GOT SPEED?

Now that we have explored melodic and rhythmic speed exercises, let's take a look at more traditional chromatic alternate-picking runs. These chromatic runs are designed to focus on speed, dexterity, and stamina. Just like in the previous exercises, it is important to start out slowly and bring up the metronome steadily.

CHROMATIC ALTERNATE-PICKING EXERCISES

The following exercise uses four-note-per-string chromatic patterns and can be easily changed to fit any type of ascending or descending movement and is adaptable for seven- and eight-string guitars.

Ex. 131 Track 156

This next chromatic run is more difficult since it moves across the fretboard quicker.

Ex. 132 Track 157

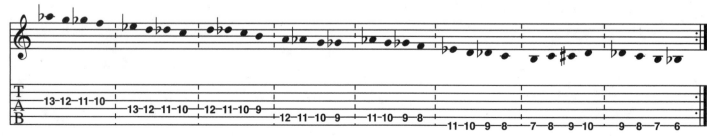

Again, make sure you start out slowly and then gradually push up your speed by 8–10 BPM. It's important that any kind of speed practice is always comfortable and musically sound and accurate.

Practice Tip

Once you reach your top speed, or plateau, subtract a few BPMs from your metronome and keep practicing at this new tempo. It is important for healthy development to always push but also to back off to let your hands catch up. By keeping track of your tempo markings, you will experience over time that your basic abilities will improve and you will have set new speed standards in your picking.

MORE CHROMATIC ALTERNATE-PICKING EXERCISES

Here are a few more chromatic speed runs.

Ex. 133 Track 158

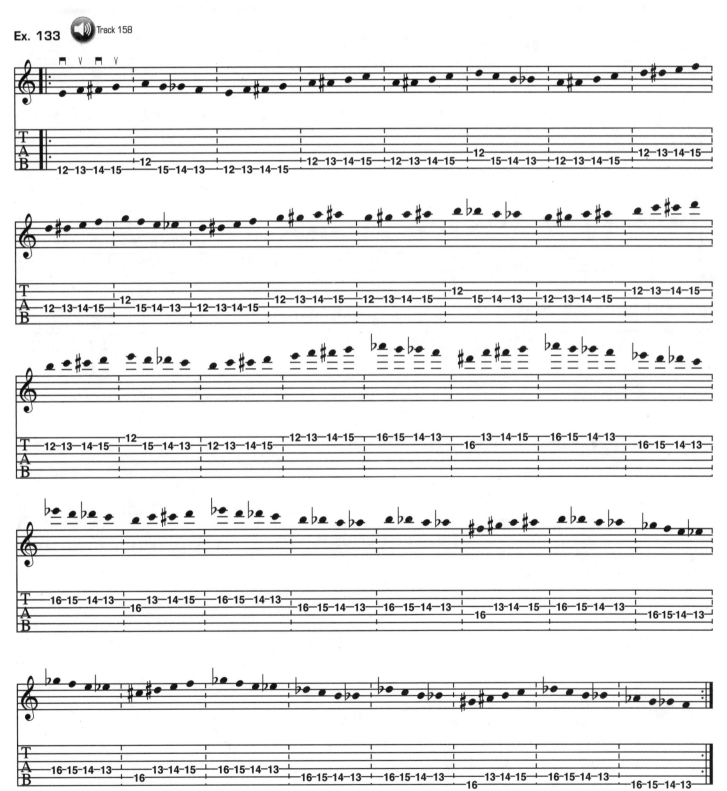

Here's one with a more-complicated rhythm. Be sure to keep it precise but fluid.

Ex. 134  Track 159

APPLICATION TIME

ETUDES FOR THE BUSY DAYS

With all these exercises and concepts, it's easy to overlook that you can also take any of these patterns and fragments, and compose short musical ideas that can function as warm-up or practice routines. Following is a collection of short etudes that increase in difficulty and can serve as a starting point for your own lines and solo ideas. As always, set your metronome to a slow tempo, and increase as your skill level and comfort grows.

Etude 1

Let's start out with some pentatonic ideas. Here's a short lick that combines two different pentatonic scales, A Minor and B Minor, with some position changes. Have fun!

Ex. 135 Track 160 Slow
Track 161 Fast

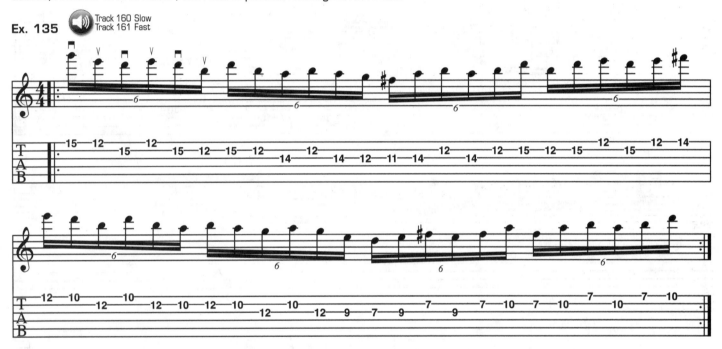

Etude 2

This next one incorporates horizontal movements and pattern combinations. Pay close attention to the position shifts.

Ex. 136 Track 162 Slow
Track 163 Fast

Etude 3

The following etude incorporates intervals and multiple pentatonic positions, and features a rhythmic twist. Take on each element separately before putting it all together.

Track 164 Slow
Track 165 Fast

Ex. 137

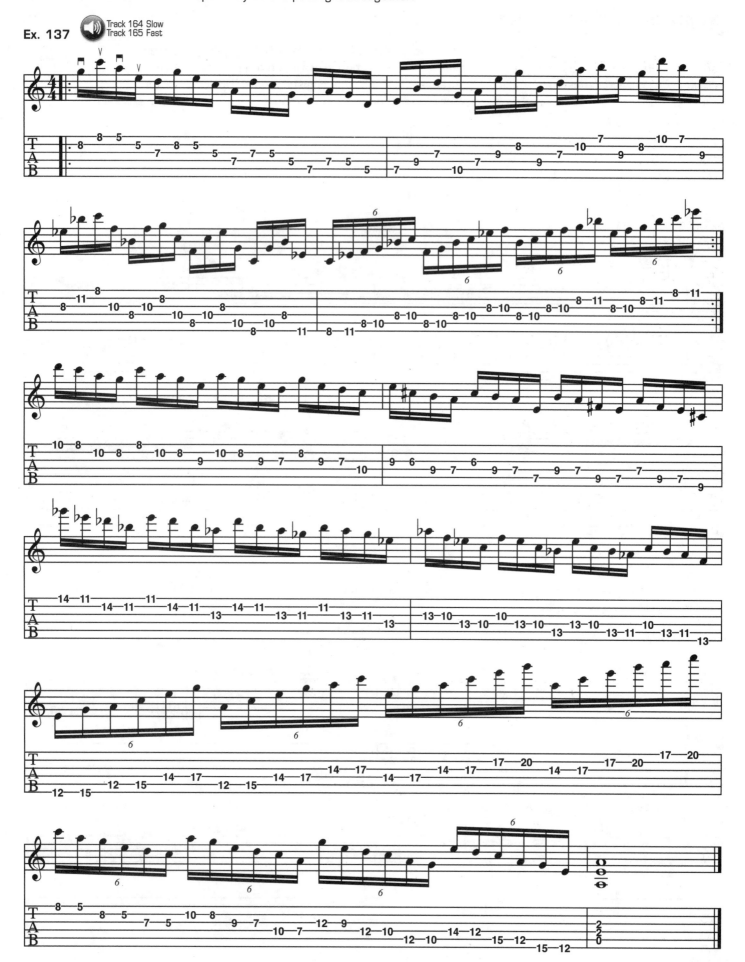

Etude 4

Etude 4 challenges you to some string skipping. Make sure to keep string noise to a minimum.

Ex. 138  Track 166 Slow
Track 167 Fast

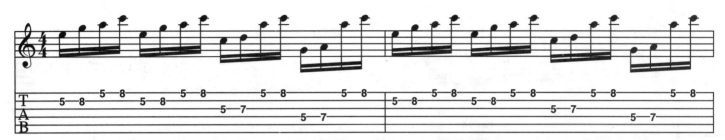

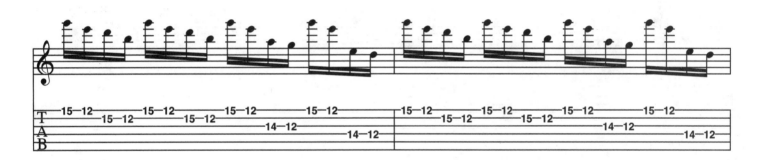

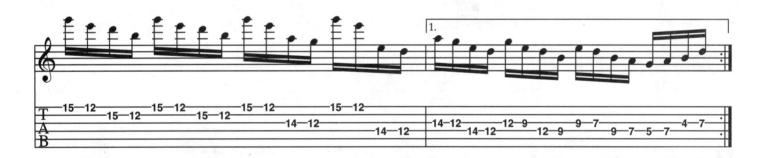

Etude 5

Now, let's take a look at some three-note-per-string etudes. Let's start out with this single- and two-string idea. You'll be applying some of the basic four-note patterns here. This is a longer etude, so make sure you memorize the different parts, and aim for a smooth tone.

Ex. 139   Track 168 Slow
Track 169 Fast

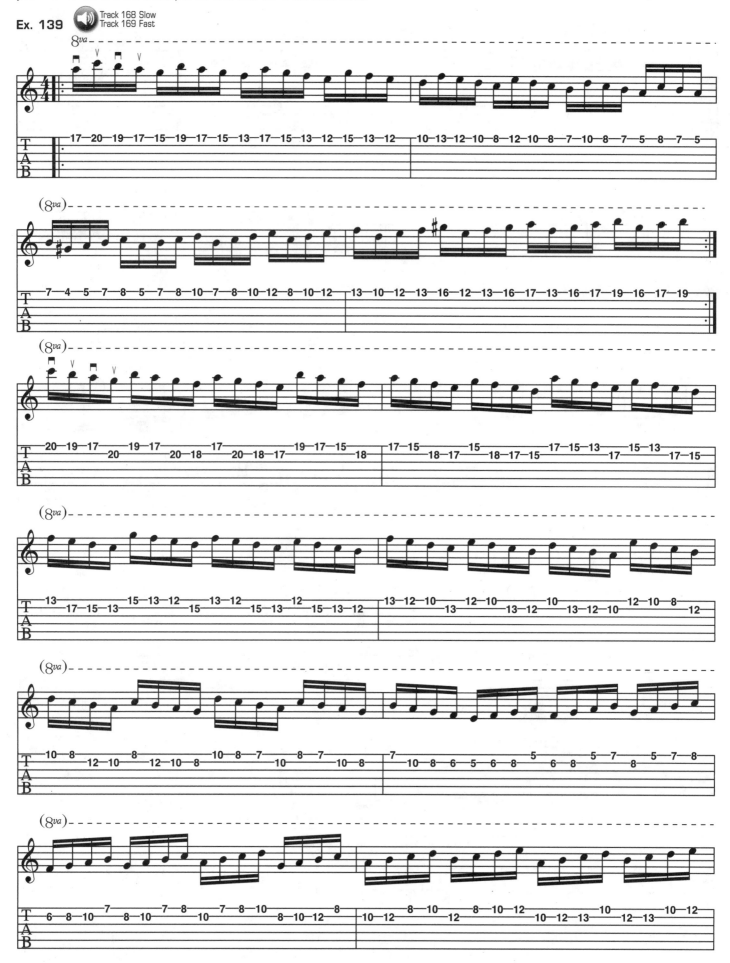

Etude 6

This one will be more challenging as it incorporates big string skips and a pedal tone. Try to memorize
the skips first.

Ex. 140

Track 170 Slow
Track 171 Fast

Etude 7

Etudes 7 and 8 will get you across the entire fretboard. Make sure to memorize the position shifts, and make the slide connections smooth.

Ex. 141 Track 172 Slow
Track 173 Fast

Etude 8

This is a variation of etude 7.

Ex. 142 Track 174 Slow
Track 175 Fast

Etude 9

This etude will get you acquainted with intervals. Make sure you are familiar with the position shifts first.
This etude includes descending 2nds, ascending 3rds, and combinations of 4ths, 5ths, 6ths, and 7ths. It
will definitely challenge you.

Ex. 143   Track 176 Slow
Track 177 Fast

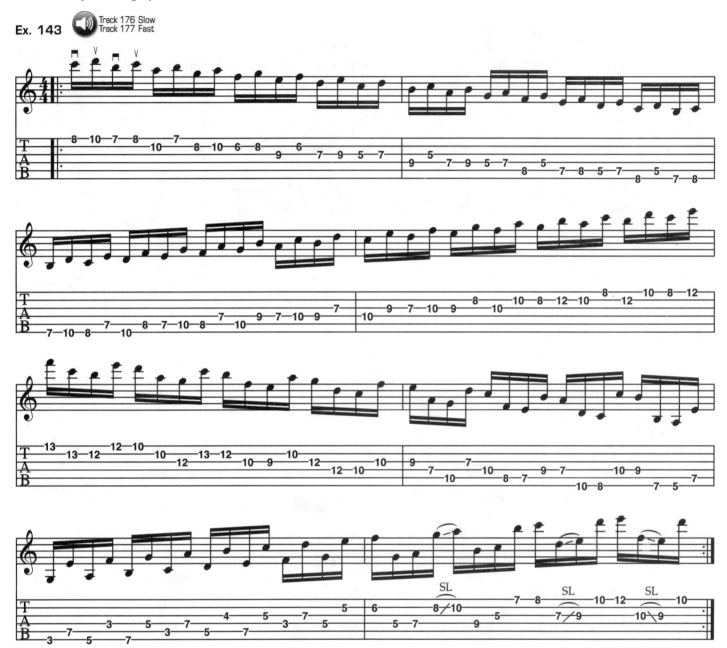

Etude 10

How about some more challenging material? This next one utilizes quintuplets and string skipping.

Ex. 144 Track 178 Slow
Track 179 Fast

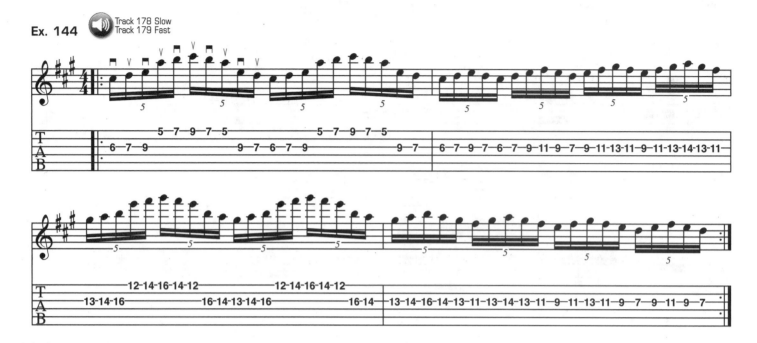

Etude 11

This one crosses from the 6th string to the 1st and then returns to its starting point.

Ex. 145 Track 180 Slow
Track 181 Fast

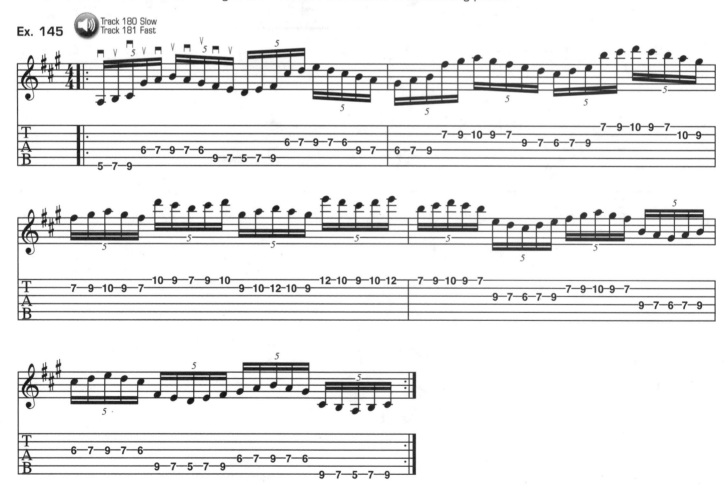

Etude 12

Etudes 12 and 13 will get you across the fretboard quickly. Make sure you memorize all the shifts, and don't lose count of the sextuplet rhythm.

Ex. 146 Track 182 Slow
Track 183 Fast

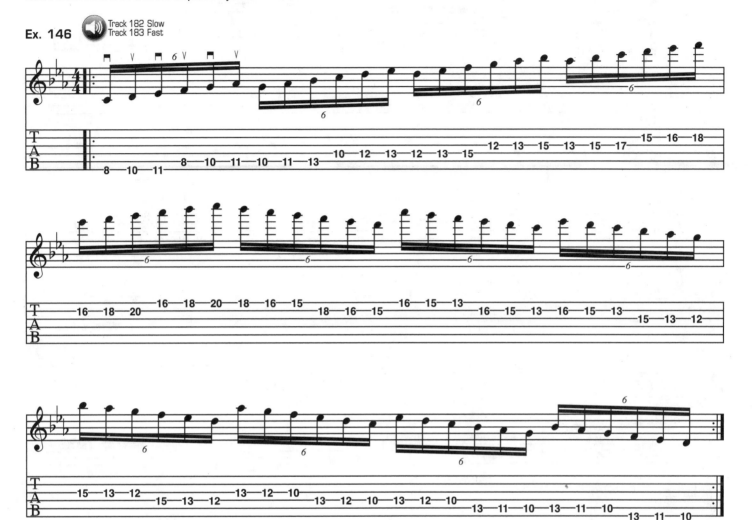

Etude 13

Ex. 147 Track 184 Slow
Track 185 Fast

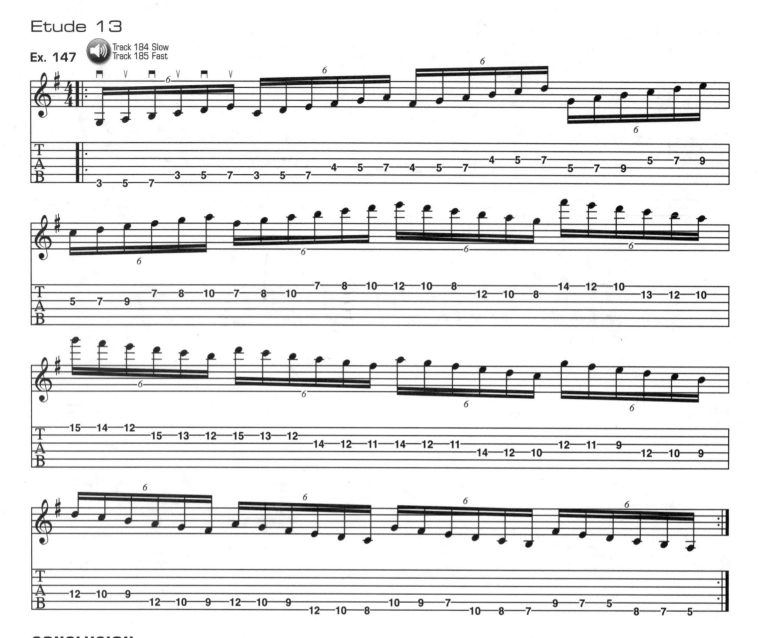

CONCLUSION

Developing picking speed can be hard work and is based on many different components. It is important that you understand how your hands work, the way you prefer to hold a pick, the type of pick you choose, and what movements you need to do smoothly and efficiently. Once you know how to use your body, you can easily work on all the challenges.

With all the exercises, scales, fragments, permutations, and more that we've covered, you are probably asking yourself, how will I get all this into my daily routine? In my experience, routine is most important and will contribute to your ability to develop picking technique and speed. Try to organize ideas and exercises into groups and little practice fragments that balance scale workouts with other topics. Now, keep changing exercises within your groups so you can cover all the patterns, scales, and other techniques within a reasonable, set practice session.

I'd recommend you practice three to four times a day in short practice sessions to keep your muscles and memory working. This may not always be possible, so find your best time to practice and make this time consistent so that you condition your body to be ready for practice time. Additionally, keep a journal to document your progress and track the material you are working on.

Now is the most important thing to remember: it's ultimately about music and about playing guitar, so it should always be fun. There's nothing better in the world than making music and playing guitar!

Pick on,
German Schauss